THE STOP SMOKING WORKBOOK

Lori Stevic-Rust, Ph.D.
& Anita Maximin, Psy.D.

MJF BOOKS
NEW YORK

Published by MJF Books
Fine Communications
Two Lincoln Square
60 West 66th Street
New York, NY 10023

The Stop Smoking Workbook
Library of Congress Catalog Card Number 96-79504
ISBN 1-56731-207-1

Copyright © 1996 by Anita Maximin, Psy.D., and Lori Stevic-Rust, Ph.D.

Text design by Tracy Marie Powell.
Illustrations by James Edmonds and by Shelby Designs and Illustrates.

This edition published by arrangement with New Harbinger Publications, Inc.

Manufactured in the United States of America on acid-free paper

MJF Books and the MJF colophon are trademarks of Fine Creative Media, Inc.

10   9   8   7   6   5   4   3   2   1

This book is dedicated to smokers and their families who are committed to a healthier, smoke-free lifestyle.

Contents

IV. Establishing a Healthy Lifestyle

V. Maintaining a Smoke-Free Lifestyle

Acknowledgments

We would like to recognize all of the smokers whom we have come in contact with who have shared their smoking experiences and their creative strategies for quitting with us.

We would like to acknowledge the companies and organizations that allowed us to assist them in their commitment to establishing a smoke-free environment.

A treatment book would not have been possible without the valuable contributions of researchers and clinicians who devote their time to studying this addiction.

In writing this book, we are indebted to Rudi Kobetic, James Edmonds, and Rockney Shepheard, for readily responding to our frantic schedules.

Our gratitude also goes to Matt McKay, Dana Landis, Kristin Beck, Gayle Zanca, Lauren Dockett, and other staff at New Harbinger for their genuine enthusiasm and warm support from the beginning of this project. In particular, our thanks go to Kirk Johnson and Nina Sonenberg, for their meticulous editing and friendly, responsive styles which made the editing process pleasurable.

And, finally, with love, we thank our families, Jay and Sarah Rust, Rudi and Vijay Kobetic, for their patience and tolerance while we completed this book. Their loving patience was particularly appreciated, given that we were both pregnant throughout this project!

I

PREPARATION FOR QUITTING

1

Introduction

"To cease smoking is the easiest thing I ever did; I ought to know because I've done it a thousand times."

—Mark Twain

If you have shared Mark Twain's sentiment at some point in your life then it may be time for you to approach the quitting process in a different way. This workbook was written to assist you in your efforts to quit smoking and to remain a non-smoker. It will help to educate yourself about the smoking habit and to learn healthy alternative strategies for your life without cigarettes.

The goal of this workbook is to guide you on your quest to improve your health and that of your friends and family. With perseverance and commitment you can become physically more fit, experience less distress, and overall feel better about yourself when you quit smoking.

A large portion of this book focuses on the issues of motivation and readiness to quit smoking. Research and clinical experience have shown that on the journey towards smoking cessation people pass through many stages of readiness. Researchers Prochaska and DiClemente and their colleagues proposed a model of this change process in 1983 which suggests that smokers initially move through a stage of **precontemplation** where the smoker is not thinking seriously about actually quitting smoking. This would include times when you may have said to yourself, "I probably should quit but I'm not ready and am not making any immediate plans to change my behavior." This is followed by a stage of **contemplation and determination** where the smoker is beginning to plan and/or to decide to quit smoking. At this stage you may have been told by others that you need to quit smoking and you may have decided it was time to make some changes in your smoking behavior. Following the contemplation phase is the **action** stage where the smoker is prepared to quit smoking and actually feels ready to set a quit date. This is that phase where you feel energized and ready to stamp out that last cigarette. Finally, smokers move into a **maintenance and/or relapse** phase. At this point some smokers maintain their abstinence while others relapse and return to smoking for some period of time. Some people consider this to be the most difficult aspect of quitting smoking. Given that relapses of some kind are normal—from taking a drag off one cigarette to returning to one's original pattern of smoking—they should be seen as opportunities to learn rather than as failures. Many smokers cycle through these stages several times before finally achieving long-term cessation.

This workbook is designed to fit with these stages of change. Take a moment right now to identify where you are in the quitting process using the Quitting Stage Chart. You'll want to know, because with each stage you can benefit from several strategies that help move you to the next stage in the quitting process. Just check which phrases sound truest for you at this moment.

Where Are You Now?

Early Stages

If you are in the early precontemplative phase, you probably would not have bought this book. However, if you do find yourself falling somewhere in the precontemplative and early contemplative stages, you will need to focus on the early chapters of the book. The first few chapters will help you identify your personal reasons for smoking and guide you in using these reasons as motivators to get you through the cessation process. Further, the initial chapters will help you understand your thoughts and the excuses you use regarding the quitting process. This is important because the perceptions that you have about your own ability to quit smoking are the building blocks for successful quitting.

The next several chapters will provide you with information on the physical effects of smoking. Up to this point in your life smoking has probably been an unconscious act that you do frequently without actually thinking about it. It is important for you to understand the actual substances that you are inhaling into your body when you smoke, and what effects these substances have on your body. This information can strengthen your motivation and commitment to quit by making you a more educated consumer of your cigarettes, and by increasing your readiness to begin the action phase and set a quit date.

For many smokers the negative health information they receive from the media, their friends, or their family is not enough to motivate them to quit smoking. Often this is because the information is impersonal. For over 30 years the Surgeon General has been insisting that cigarette smoking is dangerous to your health. Why then are people still smoking? What have smokers done with this information? *Denial.* For many smokers formal health warnings are too far removed from their own lives to make an impact. How many times have you said to yourself, "That won't happen to me," or "I physically feel fine, therefore there must not be any negative effects from *my* smoking." It is hard to think about things that may happen to you somewhere down the road. This thinking can be dangerous. The reality is that even if you are young and healthy at this moment your smoking is setting you up for

Quitting Stage Chart

You have no plans at least within the next year to quit smoking.

Precontemplation

Others are telling you to quit but you're not ready to hear it.

You are interested in gathering information about quitting smoking.

Contemplation

You are beginning to think about quitting smoking.

You are willing to make plans to quit in the next six months.

You are willing to make some changes in your smoking behavior, such as cutting back on cigarettes in certain situations.

You are starting to motivate yourself to quit.

You are ready to quit smoking *now*.

You are willing to set a quit date within the next several weeks.

You are willing to learn new coping strategies.

Action

You are willing to make lifestyle changes.

You are ready to put up with short-term discomfort in exchange for long-term benefit.

You have already quit smoking within the past six months.

You are interested in preventing relapse and maintaining your smoke-free lifestyle.

Maintenance/Relapse

You quit smoking within the last six months but you are now smoking again.

physical consequences ... maybe sooner than you realize. For this reason, chapter 5 will provide you with a Smoking Health Questionnaire for you to use when you visit your health care provider. The questions are designed to elicit more specific information from your physician regarding your own personal health as it relates to your smoking. The goal is to make the general negative health message that you have heard about smoking more specific to you and your health.

Action

If you are in the action phase, it will still be important for you to read the early chapters to strengthen your motivation. The difference is that you will be ready to establish a quit date in the immediate future, probably within the next several weeks. After your motivation and commitment to the quitting process have been established and strengthened, it is time to move on to examining your own personal smoking habit. Everybody smokes for different reasons and uses cigarettes in different ways. For this reason, it is important for you to become more familiar with your own habit of smoking, including finding out how it started and what keeps it going. Since cigarettes have been such a part of your life they have probably become linked with many activities, feelings, and situations. For example, cigarettes may be associated with ending a meal, or used when you feel depressed, angry, or bored. These associations need to be broken for you to succeed at quitting smoking. The next several chapters will guide you through an identification of your habit, will provide you with exercises to help break your smoking associations, and will provide you with alternative coping strategies.

Finally, the last several chapters will walk you through the actual quitting process. They will help you identify a date to schedule your quitting and provide you with techniques to manage the first few weeks after you quit smoking. Quitting smoking can be a physically and emotionally difficult process. The goal is to provide you with healthy strategies to nurture and care for yourself throughout the immediate and long-term phases of the quitting process. These techniques include strategies to distract yourself, to change your thinking regarding any potential physical discomfort, and to reinforce your support systems.

Relapse

If you are in the relapse stage because you have made several prior attempts at quitting but have slipped back into smoking, you will need to focus on the early chapters. Chances are you need to re-examine your motivators for quitting. Also you will need to pay special attention to chapter 19 on relapse and all of Section II on alternative coping strategies. These chapters will help you identify your "high risk" situations and teach you healthy alternative approaches to prevent relapse from recurring.

As you work your way through this book keep in mind that quitting smoking is a *process*. It is a process that requires a series of changes in behavior and attitude over time which ultimately will lead to your goal of becoming a non-smoker. Throughout this process there may be periods of discouragement, sadness, frustration, and potential relapse. This relapse may be because you have lost sight of your commitment and motivators for change, or because you are still in the process of learning alternative strategies of coping without cigarettes. You may relapse because your support systems were not strengthened prior to quitting, or for any combination of reasons. As with anything that requires commitment, perseverance, and the need for lifestyle changes, the potential to relapse back to your "old habit" is possible. Therefore, the last chapter of the book will address ways to minimize your risk for relapse. There's still plenty you can do if you do have a slip back to smoking.

2

Facts and Myths of the Smoking Habit

Cigarette smoking has probably been a part of your life for quite some time. Do you really know much about it, though? Sometimes notions and beliefs about something, including smoking, are repeated so often that you come to believe that they are facts. For example, how often do you hear people say "they say" or "that's the way it has always been" when they are discussing certain topics? Sometimes these so-called facts or myths can be misleading, and can contribute to uninformed choices or high risk behaviors. How much do *you* really know about cigarette smoking?

See for yourself in the quiz, below. It is designed to test your knowledge and beliefs regarding the smoking habit. Answer all questions by circling either true or false.

Quiz

True/False

1. There are 40 known substances in cigarette smoke.   T   F

2. Smoking is the single major cause of fires in the United States.   T   F

3. Cigarette smoking is a major cause of coronary heart disease.   T   F

4. Economic consequences of smoking include 16 million dollars in direct medical costs each year in the United States.   T   F

5. Physical withdrawal symptoms from nicotine last six months.   T   F

Quiz (continued)

6. Most smokers gain a significant amount of weight after quitting smoking. T F

7. Nicotine is an addicting drug similar to heroin. T F

8. Your "smoker's cough" is your body's way of healing itself. T F

9. Smokers need to smoke for many years in large quantities for physical damage to occur. T F

10. Damage to the body due to cigarette smoke is always irreversible. T F

11. Most smokers quit smoking on their *first* attempt. T F

12. If you are not currently experiencing any medical problems, smoking is not physically harmful to you. T F

13. Children of smokers are at an increased risk for upper respiratory tract infections, middle ear infections, asthma, and tonsillitis. T F

14. There are no long-term effects of being exposed to cigarette smoke as a child. T F

15. It is not necessary to quit smoking completely when chewing nicotine gum or using a nicotine patch. T F

16. If you have not been smoking for several months it is safe to have an occasional cigarette. T F

17. Smoking can decrease the effectiveness of many drugs. T F

18. Smokers have twice the risk of developing infections after surgery when compared to non-smokers. T F

19. Smokers who quit smoking at least six months prior to having surgery significantly decrease their chances for developing breathing complications. T F

20. The worst dental problems associated with smoking are bad breath and brown teeth. T F

Quiz Answers

Keep track of your score for your own information. Note which answers, if any, surprise you.

1. There are 40 known substances in cigarette smoke.

   False. There are more than 4,000 identified substances.

2. Smoking is the single major cause of fires in the United States.

   True. One-third of all apartment and hotel fires are caused by smoking. Seventeen percent of private dwelling fires are caused by smoking. The result of these fires is 4,000 injuries and 1,500 deaths each year.

3. Cigarette smoking is a major cause of coronary heart disease.

   True. One-half million Americans die each year of coronary heart disease, of which 30 percent is caused by smoking.

4. Economic consequences of smoking include 16 million dollars in direct medical costs each year in the United States.

   False. Direct medical costs are about 16 billion dollars with an additional 37 billion in indirect costs related to increased morbidity, disability, and premature deaths.

5. Physical withdrawal symptoms from nicotine last six months.

   False. Physical symptoms last approximately 3 to 10 days.

6. Most smokers gain a significant amount of weight after quitting smoking.

   False. One-third of all ex-smokers gain on average three to seven pounds due to changes in the way their bodies metabolize food. An individual would need to gain 70 pounds to equal some of the harmful physical effects of smoking.

7. Nicotine is an addicting drug similar to heroin.

   True.

8. Your "smoker's cough" is your body's way of healing itself.

   False. When an individual is still smoking the "cough" loosens mucous which protects the lung and consequently exposes the lung to infection and cancer causing agents.

   True. When an individual is *not* smoking the "cough" is an attempt by the lungs to heal in the absence of chemicals.

9. Smokers need to smoke for many years in large quantities for physical damage to occur.

   False. All smoking is potentially damaging to the body. Genetic risk factors contribute to the amount and type of damage that occurs.

10. Damage to the body due to cigarette smoke is always irreversible.

   False. The amount of healing that the body will undergo after cessation of smoking depends on the amount and type of damage that has been done as well as your own individual risk factors for certain diseases.

11. Most smokers quit smoking on their *first* attempt.

   False. Many smokers attempt to quit smoking several times before they finally achieve success.

12. If you are not currently experiencing any medical problems, smoking is not physically harmful to you.

   False. With each cigarette that you inhale you take into your bloodstream thousands of poisons. Many of these are cancer-causing agents. The inhalation of these substances plus your genetic predisposition may cause multiple illnesses.

13. Children of smokers are at an increased risk for upper respiratory tract infections, middle ear infections, asthma, and tonsillitis.

   True.

14. There are no long-term effects of being exposed to cigarette smoke as a child.

   False. A recent study has found that approximately 17 percent of lung cancer cases in non-smokers can be attributed to their exposure to cigarette smoke when they were children.

15. It is not necessary to quit smoking completely when chewing nicotine gum or using a nicotine patch.

   False. The nicotine gum and patch were both designed to provide your body with a specific amount of nicotine which is to be tapered down in amount over time. The goal of these products is to ease smokers through the physical withdrawal process. When you use these products in combination with smoking you are actually increasing the amount of nicotine that your body is receiving, as well as its harmful effects.

16. If you have not been smoking for several months it is safe to have an occasional cigarette.

   False. The majority of smokers who relapse report that they felt they could have *just* one cigarette without harm. However, the *one* cigarette will generally lead to one more and over varying time periods most smokers find themselves smoking approximately the same amount.

17. Smoking can decrease the effectiveness of many drugs.

   True.

18. Smokers have twice the risk of developing infections after surgery when compared to non-smokers.

   True.

19. Smokers who quit smoking at least six months prior to having surgery significantly decrease their chances for developing breathing complications.

    True.

20. The worst dental problems associated with smoking are bad breath and brown teeth.

    False. In addition to bad breath and brown teeth, smokers are also at risk for developing cancer of the mouth, tongue, lips, and pharynx. Each year, more than 8,350 people in the United States die of oral cancer directly related to tobacco.

3

Laying the Foundation for
Successful Quitting

Who would you predict to be most successful in their efforts to quit smoking? Mark your predictions on the scale following each example.

Tom begins each morning by rolling over in bed and reaching for the pack of cigarettes on the night table. He proceeds to smoke two cigarettes, one right after the other, before getting out of bed. He then begins his morning routine (teeth brushing, shaving, etc.). Each activity is performed with a cigarette. Throughout the day Tom continues to light up a cigarette with every activity, both rest and work. Tom generally smokes at least two cigarettes when he is in the car, on the phone, or drinking coffee.

Extremely Successful	*Moderately Successful*		*Unable to Quit Smoking*
4	3	2	1

Jane is a physician at a large metropolitan hospital. She describes herself as a nervous person who tends to experience a lot of stress throughout her working day. Although she intellectually understands the dangers associated with smoking she finds herself reaching for a cigarette to calm and relax her. She rationalizes this behavior by saying to herself that this will be her last one.

Extremely Successful	*Moderately Successful*		*Unable to Quit Smoking*
4	3	2	1

Sam, a retired auto worker, complains of too much spare time. He reports an increase in his desire for a cigarette when he feels bored. He notices himself reaching for cigarettes to pass the time.

Extremely Successful	*Moderately Successful*		*Unable to Quit Smoking*
4	3	2	1

Sue has always had a "hot temper." She describes herself as "quick to anger." When she feels her anger increasing she automatically reaches for a cigarette to provide herself with "distance and cooling off time." This behavior occurs not only at work but at home as well.

Extremely Successful	Moderately Successful		Unable to Quit Smoking
4	3	2	1

Although you may have your own bias about who would be more successful in the process of quitting smoking, the reality is that the key factor identified both clinically and through research is *motivation*. Only motivation separates those who successfully quit smoking from those who do not. Therefore, it is important to understand what motivation is and is not, and how you can strengthen your own motivation for quitting.

Motivation

You may have impulsively decided to quit smoking in the past and just thrown your cigarettes away. However, what you may have discovered after a few hours, days, weeks, or even months is that you returned to smoking. Quitting should not be an impulsive decision but rather a process that requires adequate preparation in order to lay the foundation for successful cessation. Without good preparation you may set yourself up for personal failure and subsequently may become reluctant to attempt quitting again, or even believe that you are not capable of quitting.

The first step in preparing yourself to quit smoking is to examine your motivation more directly. Motivation forms the basis of your commitment to stop smoking. Willpower, guts, strength, intestinal fortitude—these are all words that have been used by smokers when describing what it takes to quit smoking. Although quitting smoking for a lifetime does require strength and commitment, understanding the *source* of one's "willpower" or motivating reasons for quitting is an important first step. Recently, smokers have been bombarded by messages to quit smoking. Cigarette costs continue to rise, places where smoking is allowed have been limited, and socially smoking has become less acceptable. However, these reasons alone are often not enough to motivate smokers to quit. It is necessary to identify your own personal reasons for wanting to quit smoking, and to evaluate the importance of these reasons. Use the exercise on page 17 to begin identifying your personal reasons for needing to quit. If your reasons for needing to quit smoking *equal* your desire to continue smoking, your chances of successfully quitting are lower. But the more weight you can truthfully put on the "quitting" side, the more the scale tips toward a smoke-free life that's right for you.

Reaffirming Motivation

On a separate index card or sheet of paper rewrite your reasons for *needing* to quit. Carry this list with you in your pocket. Place it on your refrigerator. Display it in any area that will serve to remind and motivate you throughout the process of quitting smoking. Just

Exercise

1. On the next page, begin by listing on the left side of the scale all your reasons for wanting to smoke. Be as specific as you can be. (See example.) On the right side of the scale list all the reasons why you *need* to quit smoking. Be specific.

2. Now compare each side of your scale. If your reasons for wanting to quit outweigh your reasons for why you continue to smoke, you are ready to begin the process of cessation. If your scale is fairly balanced, you need to re-examine your commitment and desire to the quitting process. As you work your way through this book, continue to add reasons to *quit* to the right side of the scale. Don't worry if the scale threatens to tip over!

Example:

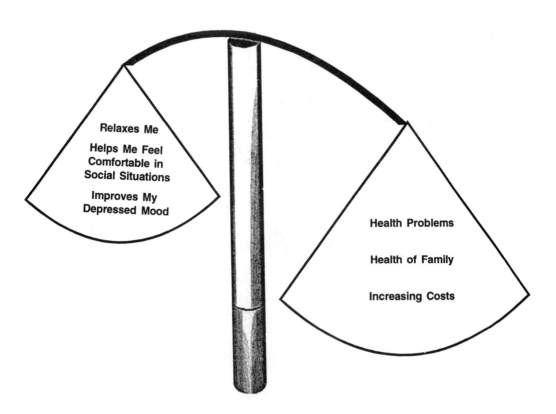

Relaxes Me

Helps Me Feel Comfortable in Social Situations

Improves My Depressed Mood

Health Problems

Health of Family

Increasing Costs

Your Balance Scale

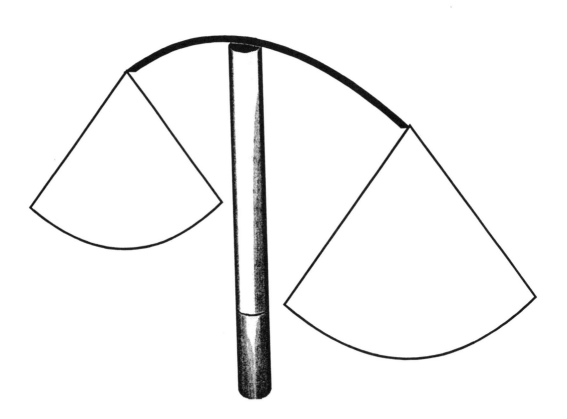

as reaching for matches or a lighter has become a habit, make a new habit of checking your list as soon as the urge to smoke hits. Write your reasons as persuasively as you can. For instance, write your children's names, or note a specific goal you can reach if you save $25.00 a week.

Sample Index Card

Improve my breathing
Improve Billy's health
Save money toward plane tickets to Paris in the spring

Don't worry if this step alone doesn't lead you to quit. It helps chip away at the unconsciousness of your smoking habit, and prepares you for the steps that follow.

Personal Excuses

Now that you have examined your personal reasons for wanting to quit, it's time to face something that many smokers do to undermine their own motivation to quit: *make excuses.* Every smoker at one time or another has used excuses to put off quitting. Excuses provide you with reasons to self-medicate with nicotine when quitting seems hard to bear. If you know and understand your own excuses, you will be empowered to alter those excuses with more healthy statements to yourself. Positive messages to yourself will help tremendously in keeping your motivation up. The following section offers samples of such messages. Try to find alternative statements that make sense to *you.*

How many of these excuses have you used?

Excuse: This is a bad time to quit because I have too many stressors in my life.
Alternative Statement: There will always be stressors in my life. This is a good opportunity to learn how to cope in a more healthy way while experiencing this stress.

Excuse: Quitting isn't worth the suffering.
Alternative Statement: The short-term discomfort that I may experience will only last up to a week and then my body will begin to heal. Quitting smoking now will minimize my risk for long-term suffering with other smoking-related diseases.

Excuse: I'm too young to have any real damage to my body. I'll quit in a couple of years.
Alternative Statement: I may not be physically experiencing the effects of my smoking but with each cigarette I deposit thousands of cancer-causing agents in my bloodstream. I am setting myself up for future physical problems.

Excuse: If I do quit I will gain a lot of weight.
Alternative Statement: Weight gain caused by changes in the body after quitting smoking averages three to seven pounds. I can control weight gain through exercise and snacking on healthy foods. Quitting smoking is the best thing I can do for my health *and* my appearance.

Excuse: It is probably too late for me to quit because too much damage has already occurred.
Alternative Statement: It is never too late to quit smoking. Immediately after I quit smoking my body will begin to heal. My breathing should improve, I'll cough less, my sense of taste and smell will return to normal, and I will reduce my risk for developing further medical problems.

Excuse: I've tried to quit before but I always fail.
Alternative Statement: It often takes smokers several attempts before they actually quit smoking. With each attempt I will learn what my "high risk" situations are and what causes me to reach for a cigarette. I will then know more about my habit for the next attempt at quitting.

Excuse: I need to smoke to calm my nerves.
Alternative Statement: Nicotine is actually a stimulant which means it arouses the nervous system. There are other things I can learn to use to calm my nerves. For example, I can take a walk or use relaxation exercises.

Excuse: I need to smoke to feel comfortable in social situations.
Alternative Statement: There are other techniques I can use to make myself feel more comfortable such as carrying my keys to occupy my hands.

Excuse: I can't quit now because I get very irritable and I don't want to get into trouble at home or at work.
Alternative Statement: This irritability is short term. People frequently get irritable or crabby and they don't reach for a cigarette. I will elicit my co-workers' support in my efforts to quit.

Excuse: It hasn't really been proven that cigarette smoking is a cause of cancer.
Alternative Statement: This is not true. Cigarette smoking is the leading cause of preventable cancer.

Excuse: I enjoy smoking too much to give it up.
Alternative Statement: The temporary enjoyment that I get is leading me closer and closer to potential long-term suffering.

Review these excuses and add others that may be more personal to you. Write your alternative statements as persuasively and accurately as you can. Remember these excuses only serve to undermine your motivation and ability to quit smoking.

Excuse:
Alternative Statement:

Excuse:
Alternative Statement:

Excuse:
Alternative Statement:

Self-Efficacy

When thinking about quitting smoking, many people make the mistake of assuming that all it will take to stay off cigarettes is willpower or motivation. How many times have you said to yourself something like, "I just need to be strong to beat the urge to smoke"? The problem with this demand is that it implies that strength of will or motivation is all that is necessary to be smoke-free. But as you may know, many people have quit for a short period of time only to find themselves smoking again. Does this mean that they have lost their willpower or motivation? Not exactly. As you saw in the previous section, being motivated to quit and making a strong commitment to change are extremely important. But people also need to *believe* that they can or know how to cope with situations that will tempt them to smoke. A researcher named Albert Bandura referred to this belief as *self-efficacy*.

Consider self-efficacy as it relates to your preparation to quit smoking. You can think of self-efficacy as your judgment of your ability to cope with a specific "high risk" situation. How much confidence do you have in your ability to resist smoking in the situations that you find most tempting? This is not to be confused with self-esteem (what you think of yourself overall). People can feel very positive about themselves but still judge themselves as not able to do a certain thing like quit smoking. Someone with a low sense of self-efficacy, who has doubts about his or her abilities in particular situations, may tend to give up more easily when faced with situations that are really tempting. Simply exerting your willpower to resist smoking in such cases isn't enough; you must believe that you can *do* something to resist, and that you know *how* to do it. As you work through this book, you will learn several techniques to help you resist the urge to smoke.

Your sense of self-efficacy is influenced by a few factors. The first is how many successes or failures you may have had when trying to quit. If you have quit smoking in the past but gave in early because you were faced with stressful situations, you may feel *less* able to quit again. You may feel less confident, saying "I can't handle this." You may feel overcome with a craving to reach for a cigarette. As a smoker you may have come to *believe* that cigarettes help you cope.

People often rely on how they feel physically to determine whether they can cope with a stressful situation. The more tense or nervous you are, the more out of control you may feel and therefore less able to resist the urge to smoke. This book will present you with other options to cope with these feelings.

Self-Efficacy Evaluation

How strongly do *you* believe in your ability to quit smoking and to manage high risk smoking situations? Circle the number corresponding to how you feel about each statement.

- My last attempt at quitting smoking failed therefore I am afraid to try again.

Strongly Agree	*Agree*	*Disagree*	*Strongly Disagree*
1	2	3	4

- I believe that I am unable to tolerate any discomfort related to quitting.

Strongly Agree	*Agree*	*Disagree*	*Strongly Disagree*
1	2	3	4

- I believe that my smoking is more powerful than I am.

Strongly Agree	*Agree*	*Disagree*	*Strongly Disagree*
1	2	3	4

- I worry that nervousness or stress will overcome me and make it impossible to quit.

Strongly Agree	*Agree*	*Disagree*	*Strongly Disagree*
1	2	3	4

- I don't believe that I personally have what it takes to quit smoking.

Strongly Agree	*Agree*	*Disagree*	*Strongly Disagree*
1	2	3	4

- I am not strong enough to use alternative strategies to cope.

Strongly Agree	*Agree*	*Disagree*	*Strongly Disagree*
1	2	3	4

- I doubt my ability to manage my life without cigarettes.

Strongly Agree	*Agree*	*Disagree*	*Strongly Disagree*
1	2	3	4

- The next time I get really angry or upset, I will definitely need a cigarette.

Strongly Agree	*Agree*	*Disagree*	*Strongly Disagree*
1	2	3	4

If you answered mostly 3's and 4's, you have a strong belief in your ability to cope with situations without smoking. This will help you when you are faced with a particularly challenging situation. Remind yourself that you *are* capable. If you answered mostly 1's and 2's, you may be doubting your abilities to manage your life without cigarettes. The following are things you can do to improve your belief in your ability to quit smoking.

1. **Learn new coping strategies,** one of the end results of having worked through this workbook. Once you arm yourself with new ways of coping instead of smoking, you will increase your confidence in your ability to quit smoking.

2. **Observe your friends and family members' attempts** in order to develop your confidence. Follow the example of someone who has quit to maintain faith and to learn how to cope more effectively with the urge to smoke. You may be motivated to stop smoking from constant pressure from others, but this in itself won't help you as much as a successful role model to remain smoke-free.

3. **Review your healthy alternative statements to yourself.** If any fail to convince you, rewrite them when you're at your most disgusted with smoking.

4. **Focus on being successful.** Imagine yourself as a non-smoker, in control of your ability to use healthy coping strategies.

5. **Remember that quitting smoking is a process** and as such may take several attempts. Don't interpret past attempts as failures, but rather as learning opportunities.

6. **Quitting smoking may seem like one of the most difficult things that you will do** but remember that with practice you will succeed. The challenge will let you feel that much better about your ability to remain a non-smoker.

4

Anatomy of the Smoking Process

The goal of this chapter is to make your smoking a more conscious and informed act. If you actually think about the content of what you are inhaling into your body, and the effect that these substances are having on your immediate and long-term health, the "pleasure" of smoking dwindles—sometimes to a vanishing point. At the same time you increase your desire and motivation to quit smoking.

In the second chapter you were given a quiz on facts and myths regarding the cigarette habit. One of the questions asked you to speculate on how many substances have been identified in cigarettes and cigarette smoke. Did you guess more than 4,000? Was your guess significantly lower? Most smokers are shocked to discover how *many* substances they are inhaling and equally stunned at *what* these substances are.

Smokers have been informed that cigarettes contain carbon monoxide, tar, and nicotine. This information is reported on the side of a pack of cigarettes and included in cigarette advertisements. However, information regarding the other 4,000 substances has not been readily available to the general smoking population. In a 1992 study, 85 percent of the smokers surveyed said that they believed smokers should be informed about the other toxic substances found in cigarettes. Further, approximately 67 percent of these smokers reported that if they knew that cigarettes contained asbestos, arsenic, DDT, and lead they would be more motivated to quit. Therefore, this next section aims to provide you with a brief list of substances included in the 4,000 figure. This is in keeping with this book's general goal of making you a more educated consumer of smoking. Step by step your smoking will become a more conscious act and less of a *habit*.

Following the Smoke

What actually happens in your body when you inhale your cigarette? Do you know? Would knowing this information change your motivation about smoking? Would it affect the "pleasure" of your smoking habit if you visualized what is happening in your body at the moment you inhaled? Many smokers report that they tend to ignore or to deny the harmful negative

Did You Know?

Substance	Description	Effect on the Body	Cancer-Causing Agent	Tumor Initiator Agent	Toxic Agent
tar	black sticky substance	adheres to the lungs and makes it difficult to breathe		*	
arsenic	poisonous gas				*
ammonia	powerful substance found in cleaning agents	irritant to throat and nasal passages			
carbon monoxide	gas that is emitted from car exhaust pipe	poisons healthy red blood cells limiting the amount of oxygen to organs		*	
hydrogen cyanide	substance used in gas chamber to kill	toxic to cilia in the lungs, limiting their ability to clear poisons from the lungs	*	*	
formaldehyde	substance used to embalm dead bodies				
asbestos	fiber-like substance used for insulating, now banned	adheres to the lungs	*		
PO210	radioactive substance found in fertilizers used on tobacco		*		
cyanide	deadly poison				
lead	substance that has been banned from paint and plumbing	associated with neurological damage			
DDT	deadly pesticide	poison	*		
acetaldehyde	first degree metabolite of ethanol	affects the heart			

effects that cigarettes have on their body because it makes continued smoking much easier. For example, would you be able to enjoy and relax when smoking your cigarette if at the same time you were envisioning black, sticky tar adhering to your lungs, or carbon monoxide limiting the oxygen to your brain? If you are like most smokers the answer is probably no. In order to continue smoking despite all the health consequences, you have to push that information out of your awareness. Therefore, the act of quitting smoking requires that you make every drag off your cigarette something that you are fully aware of, envisioning its track inside your body.

Imagine if your body were transparent and you could see all your organs and blood vessels. The following exercise is designed to help you visualize your own body and what happens during smoking. The graphic designs are separated into each of the primary areas or systems within your body affected by smoking. It's time to take a journey through your body as if you could watch the toxic substances as they enter and leave each system. Although this can be frightening and even overwhelming, the purpose of this exercise is again to make you a more educated and conscious consumer of your cigarettes.

Healthy Body Systems

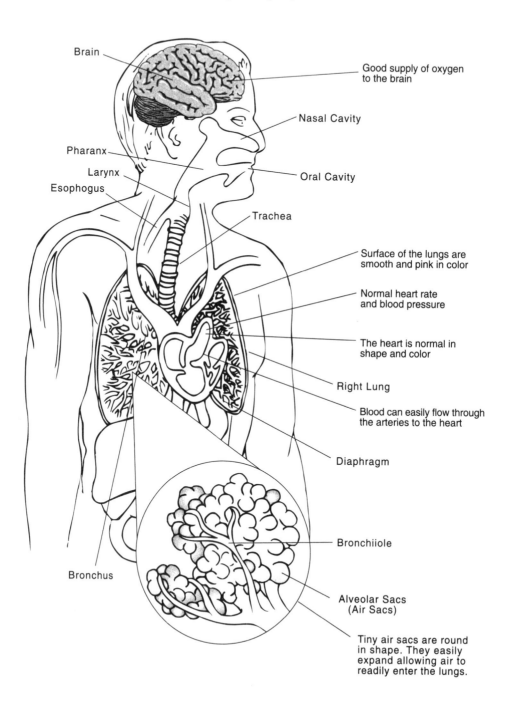

Brain

Good supply of oxygen to the brain

Nasal Cavity

Pharanx

Larynx

Esophogus

Oral Cavity

Trachea

Surface of the lungs are smooth and pink in color

Normal heart rate and blood pressure

The heart is normal in shape and color

Right Lung

Blood can easily flow through the arteries to the heart

Diaphragm

Bronchus

Bronchiiole

Alveolar Sacs (Air Sacs)

Tiny air sacs are round in shape. They easily expand allowing air to readily enter the lungs.

Pulmonary System (Your Lungs)

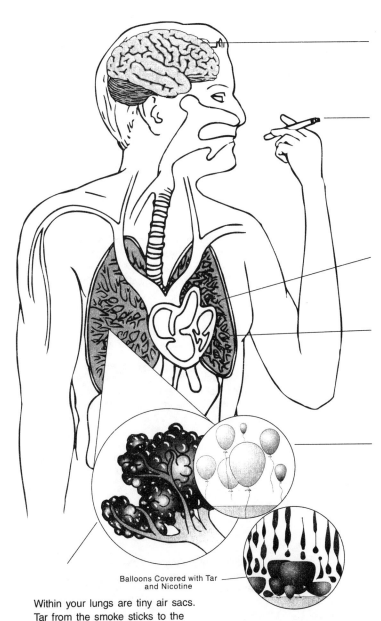

Within seven seconds after you inhale your cigarette, nicotine has entered your brain. Carbon monoxide enters the brain and limits the oxygen supply.

Smoke acts as an irritant to your nose and mouth.

Within three seconds after you inhale your cigarette, nicotine has entered your bloodstream.

Now the smoke enters your lungs where 90 percent of the dangerous substances are absorbed.

Your lungs begin to look black and deformed from the substances you inhale. Try exhaling the smoke from your cigarette into a white handkerchief. What you see on there is what your lungs look like.

These air sacs are as fragile as balloons. When this heavy sticky tar gets on them it makes it difficult for them to take in and let out air. This makes it difficult for you to breathe.

Balloons Covered with Tar
and Nicotine

Within your lungs are tiny air sacs. Tar from the smoke sticks to the sacs. This causes the sacs to become deformed in shape, lose their elasticity, and prevent air from easily entering your lungs.

Cardiovascular System (Your Heart)

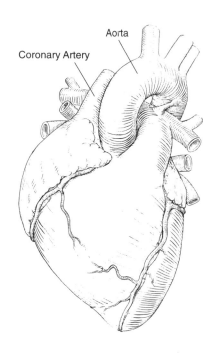

Coronary Artery

Aorta

Immediately after you inhale your cigarette your blood pressure increases by 10 to 20 points.

Blood vessels in the brain can become clogged and stop blood flow which can result in a stroke.

The heart can become discolored from the black tar.

This increase in your heart rate and blood pressure increases your body's need for oxygen and therefore your heart must work much harder.

Although your body needs more oxygen, the carbon monoxide from your cigarette decreases the amount of oxygen that can get into your body. This can lead to chest pain or heart attack.

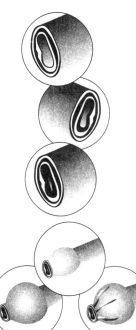

The cigarette smoke can contribute to the formation of cholesterol and other fatty substances on the inside lining of the arteries in your heart.

This leads to a narrowing or closing off of blood flow to the heart. This can lead to a heart attack.

When your blood pressure increases, the strain on your arteries is great.

Not only is blood trying to pass through a narrow opening, but it is doing so under great pressure.

This can result in the artery rupturing and bleeding.

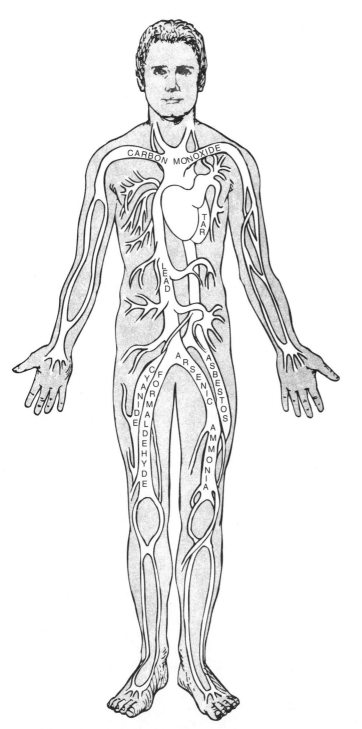

Over 4,000 dangerous substances are flowing through your body.

They are being carried in your blood to all organ systems in your body.

They touch the mouth, nose, esophagus, stomach, kidney, liver, bladder, pancreas, etc.

All of the organs of the body are exposed to cancer-causing agents.

No part of the body remains untouched by the smoke.

5

Your Personal Smoking Health

It is often difficult to believe the negative health messages that you hear, particularly if you feel in good health. You are not necessarily healthy simply because you are not currently experiencing symptoms or consider yourself sick. Early recognition of potential threats to your health is one of the best defenses against illness. How often have you said to yourself or heard other smokers say, "I know smoking isn't good for me but I feel fine," or "I smoke but I can still run five miles a day," or "My grandfather smoked and he lived to 80 years old." These statements reflect a true lack of information about one's own health and personal vulnerabilities to smoking. In order to make a truly informed choice to quit smoking, to continue to smoke, or to stay off cigarettes for a lifetime, you must obtain complete and accurate information about your health. To that end, the following reference guide has been put together for you to use when seeing your health care provider.

Remember, while you may have other risk factors for each of the described conditions, smoking remains the single greatest risk factor within your control. With a more complete understanding of your own health factors as they relate to your smoking, you are in a better position to maintain your motivation towards smoking cessation.

Make a copy of the Smoking Health Questionnaire and take it with you as a reference guide to aid in your discussion with your health care provider.

Medical Blood Tests and Procedures That Are Affected by Smoking

Smoking not only can affect the efficacy of some medication; it can also interfere with the accuracy of results on some medical tests. It is important that you notify your health care providers that you are a smoker and how much you smoke before you have blood work or other tests performed. Below is a list of some of these tests and how smoking can affect the results.

Smoking Health Questionnaire

Chronic Obstructive Pulmonary Disease (COPD) includes emphysema, bronchitis, and asthma, the fifth leading cause of death in the United States. Emphysema causes the tiny air sacs in the lungs to lose their elasticity. This in turn makes it difficult for smokers to "catch their breath." Warning signs of a loss of elasticity include when you "feel winded," or when you experience "smoker's cough." The bronchi are tubes that carry air to and from the lungs. Smoking can cause these tubes to become inflamed. This condition is called bronchitis. Asthma is characterized by a narrowing of the airways in the lungs which makes it difficult to breathe. While some damage to the lungs from emphysema cannot be cured, other symptoms related to bronchitis and asthma can be reversed when you quit smoking.

Ask yourself:

Am I at risk for developing asthma, bronchitis, or emphysema? Are my symptoms of coughing, trouble "catching my breath" after I use the stairs, and wheezing related to my smoking?

Pneumonia and flu are the sixth leading cause of death in the United States. Smokers are at higher risk for developing these acute respiratory infections than non-smokers. This occurs because smoking prevents the cilia, which are hair-like "sweepers," to remove toxins and allergens from your lungs. This leaves the lungs susceptible to infection.

Ask yourself:

Is the frequency of my flu-like symptoms related to my smoking? Am I at greater risk for developing pneumonia?

Coronary Heart Disease. Most smokers think of smoking as causing damage only to their lungs, if anywhere. However, your heart can also be adversely affected by your smoking. Coronary heart disease is the leading cause of death in the United States. It can lead to chest pain and heart attacks. Smokers have two to four times greater incidence of developing coronary heart disease, and a 70 percent greater chance of dying from heart disease, as compared to non-smokers. Smoking requires the heart to work harder to compensate for the decrease in oxygen caused by the carbon monoxide that you inhale with each cigarette. Smoking also can lead to the formation of plaque, hard deposits of fatty tissue inside the artery. This makes it difficult for blood to flow easily through the artery.

Ask yourself:

What are my risk factors for developing coronary heart disease? Which of my cardiac symptoms are related to my smoking?

Stroke is the closing or rupturing of a blood vessel in the brain. The results of a stroke include death or brain damage including speech difficulties, memory loss, weakness or paralysis on one side of the body, etc. Smokers have twice the risk of dying from a stroke as non-smokers. After quitting smoking for several years the risk of having a stroke returns to the level of a non-smoker.

Ask yourself:

What is my risk for having a stroke?

Hypertension is the medical term for high blood pressure. If you have a problem with your blood pressure, it could be caused by your smoking or at the very least made worse by your smoking. Nicotine acts to increase blood pressure within seconds after you inhale your cigarette. Further, nicotine interferes with the efficacy of some medications used to control high blood pressure.

Ask yourself:

How does my smoking affect my blood pressure and its treatment?

Efficacy of drugs. Cigarette smoking can interfere with how efficiently some medications work. These medications include:

Propanolol	Theo-Dur
Atenolol	Nifedipine
Insulin	Inderal
Darvon	

Ask yourself:

Is any of the medication that I am taking affected by my smoking?

Diabetes is a disease affecting the secretion of insulin, which is a hormone produced by the pancreas to regulate blood sugar levels. Although diabetes is not *caused* by smoking, smoking significantly complicates your diabetic condition. Diabetes doubles the risk for stroke, peripheral vascular disease, and heart attacks. If you smoke and are diabetic you increase your risk by *four to eleven times.* Also, nicotine acts to constrict the arteries, thereby further limiting the blood supply to your extremities. This increases your risk for gangrene and the potential loss of a limb. Further, diabetics often mistakenly believe that smoking is O.K. because it helps them to control their weight. The reality is that quitting smoking can be equally important in your diabetic management.

Ask yourself:

What relationship is there between my diabetic symptoms, their management, and my smoking? How will quitting smoking reduce complications?

Ulcers. Smoking affects the development of ulcers and complicates the healing process. Nicotine appears to reduce the pressure on the sphincter muscle at the end of the esophagus. This relaxation allows the acid from your stomach to back up and cause damage to your esophagus and stomach. Smoking while you have an ulcer increases your risk to develop bleeding and slows down the healing process.

Ask yourself:

How does my smoking contribute to my gastrointestinal symptoms?

Surgery. If you require surgery, it is important to know that smoking slows the healing process, impairs the immune system, and therefore increases your risk for infection. Smoking can cause many breathing complications which increase recovery time. The breathing difficulties are related to the fact that smokers cough more and produce more sputum, while their lungs are less efficient at clearing these substances away. Also, a smoker's lung is not as efficient at exhaling anesthesia that has been inhaled. Studies have shown that quitting smoking at least *two months* before surgery reduces your chances for pulmonary complications. Quitting smoking *six months* prior to surgery gives you similar pulmonary complications odds as that of a non-smoker. Quitting at least six weeks prior to surgery allows your immune system to return to normal and therefore reduces your risks for infection.

Ask yourself:

How will my smoking interfere with my recovery from surgery? Will I have a higher risk for infection? Will I require more oxygen and experience a longer recovery time?

Red Blood Cell Count, Hematocrit, Hemoglobin

All three of these tests can tell your physician if your blood count is normal or if you could be anemic, bleeding, and so on. In a smoker these levels tend to be higher than normal, probably due to the carbon monoxide in your blood. Carbon monoxide sticks to the hemoglobin, the component responsible for carrying oxygen in the blood. This makes it difficult for oxygen to reach every area of your body. These levels can return to normal a few weeks after you quit smoking.

High-Density Lipoprotein Levels (HDL)

The HDL of a smoker tends to be lower than that of a non-smoker. HDL, the "good" cholesterol, serves a protective role for the heart. Therefore, this lower-than-normal level can potentially increase a smoker's risk for heart disease.

Serum Protein Blood Levels

The serum protein blood levels can indicate problems with the kidneys, evidence of diabetes, congestive heart failure, and impaired absorption of food from the intestines. These levels can be artificially low in smokers. Therefore, it is important that you inform your health care provider that you are a smoker and how much you smoke. This will prevent inaccurate interpretation of these test results.

Upper Gastrointestinal Series

Typically, smokers are asked to abstain from smoking for 12 hours before having an upper GI series because smoking can interfere with the test. This is probably due to the fact that smoking stimulates secretions in the stomach.

Electroencephalogram (EEG)

If you are scheduled to have an EEG, you may want to consult with your physician about what kind of smoking guidelines you should follow prior to the test. It appears that when smokers are deprived of cigarettes their alpha frequency brainwaves are decreased. This may alter the accuracy of your results.

Smoking Health of Infants and Children

If you have noticed that your children or grandchildren tend to have frequent coughs, runny noses, or ear infections, consider the possibility that your smoking is partly responsible. The questions that follow were designed to increase your understanding about "passive smoke" and how it specifically affects the health of your children. This information can provide yet another reinforcement to you that your decision and commitment to quit smoking are healthy for *everyone*. You can be proud of yourself in knowing that quitting smoking will significantly improve the health of your children. Remind yourself of this fact when the quitting process becomes difficult.

Do you have children?

What are the names and ages of your children? _____

Do you have grandchildren?

What are the names and ages of your grandchildren? _____

_____

How many colds, ear infections, and coughs do your children or grandchildren tend to have each year? _____

Do any of your children or grandchildren have asthma? _____

_____

Have your children or grandchildren had bronchitis or tonsillitis? _____

_____

_____

Do you believe that your cigarette smoke is harmful to your children or grandchildren?

When adults want to escape the harmful effects of inhaling somebody else's cigarette they can leave the room, request a different table in a restaurant, and request smokers not to smoke in their homes, cars, or offices. Unfortunately, infants and children do not have a choice about whether or not they inhale smoke from a cigarette. If you have children in your household and you smoke, you continue to expose them to the harmful effects of the smoke.

The smoke that children and other non-smokers inhale from a smoker's cigarette is called "passive smoke" or "second-hand" smoke. This smoke consists of 15 percent *mainstream* smoke and 85 percent *sidestream* smoke. Mainstream smoke includes the smoke inhaled and exhaled by the smoker. The sidestream smoke is the smoke from the burning end of the cigarette.

The Dangers of Passive Smoke for Children

The negative health consequences of passive smoke were first recognized by the Surgeon General in 1972. Since then the evidence of the adverse effects of passive smoke has continued to increase. The harmful effects are particularly noted for infants and children whose parents smoke. Below is a list of some of these harmful effects.

- The amount of carbon monoxide in the blood is 2.5 times greater in the children and infants of smokers than it is for the *actual* smoker. Carbon monoxide reduces the amount of oxygen that is available to body tissue. This reduction is linked to **poor growth and development**.

- Some researchers have discovered a link between the incidence of **Sudden Infant Death Syndrome (SIDS)** and parents who smoke in the home.

- **The incidence of middle ear infections is significantly higher** for children of smokers. Within the ear, there are tiny hair-like structures which remove or *sweep away* hazardous substances. It appears that cigarette smoke tends to damage these hair-like structures and therefore prevents the ear from removing these substances. This in turn leads to infections.

- Children and infants who are exposed to passive smoke are at greater risk for **developing bronchitis**, which is an infection of the bronchial tubes in the lungs. The same is true for **tonsillitis**, which is an inflammation of the tonsils, and **laryngitis**.

- **Pneumonia and other upper respiratory tract infections** are more common in children below the age of two of parents who smoke. This is because relative to their small body weight they end up inhaling *more* of the poisons from the smoke than the smoker does.

- There is a greater incidence for children of smokers to **develop asthma**. Moreover, these children are at greater risk for developing complications related to their asthma than asthmatic children of non-smokers.

- Children of smokers tend to lag three to five months behind their peers in reading and math abilities.

- Children of smokers have shorter attention spans, tend to be more hyperactive, and score lower in spelling than children of non-smokers.

- Relatively recent research has found that the consequences for children whose parents smoke in their presence may be long lasting. In a group of **non-smoking adults who developed lung cancer, 17 percent of these cases were attributable to exposure to cigarette smoke as a child or adolescent.**

Smoking Health of Women

When the Surgeon General's first report on the harmful effects of smoking came out in the 1960s, smoking among men began to decline. However, smoking among women continued to increase until it hit its peak in the 1970s. While the decline in smoking for men decreased from 50 percent to 32 percent between 1965 and 1987, the rate for women in this time period only declined from 32 percent to 27 percent. It is projected that if these rates continue, smoking rates between men and women will be equal by the mid-1990s. Thereafter the rate of smoking by women may surpass that of men.

Men and women share many similar health risks from smoking, including similar death rates for most smoking-related illnesses. However, there are unique areas of risk for women involving fertility, birth control, and particularly pregnancy. The benefits of quitting smoking are great for women in each of these high risk areas.

- According to the American Cancer Society, **lung cancer has now replaced breast cancer as the leading cause of death in women.**

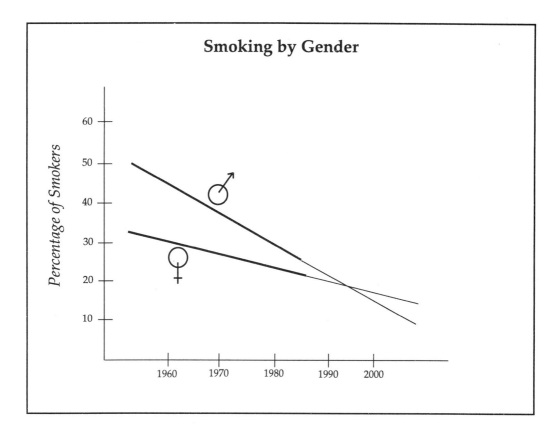

- Women who smoke have **two to three times the rate of cervical cancer** as non-smoking women.

- There is a **greater incidence of breast cancer** among women who smoke.

- Women who smoke and take birth control pills increase their risk for **developing blood clots, having a stroke, and having a heart attack, particularly if over the age of 35.**

- Smoking women have a natural **menopause one to two years earlier** than non-smoking women.

- Smoking increases the risk for developing osteoporosis, particularly in post-menopausal women. Osteoporosis is a condition that causes thinning of the bone tissue, leading to approximately 1.2 million bone fractures each year in the U.S. Many of these fractures are fatal.

- **Smoking increases the rate at which estrogen is broken down** in a woman's body. This increases the risk for osteoporosis.

- Women with osteoporosis who smoke are **three times more likely to lose their teeth in their fifties.**

Pregnancy

Women who are pregnant or thinking about becoming pregnant have an additional *tiny* reason to quit smoking. Many of the harmful effects that smoking has on you are passed on to the developing baby inside of you. In addition, there are numerous other harmful and deadly effects from your smoking on your baby. Imagine all of the poisons that you inhale into your body when you smoke. These are the same poisons that your baby is exposed to. The difference is *you* have a choice, but the growing baby inside of you does not. Quitting smoking prior to getting pregnant or as early as possible after pregnancy can greatly decrease the harmful effects on your baby. Below are a few of the important facts that you should be aware of regarding smoking while you are pregnant.

- The fertility of women who smoke is significantly reduced. That means it's harder for smokers to get pregnant in the first place.

- There are 115,000 miscarriages each year directly linked to smoking.

- Pregnant women who smoke expose their babies to carbon monoxide poisoning. The carbon monoxide in your cigarette reduces the amount of oxygen that your baby can get.

- Oxygen is also limited to the baby because nicotine constricts or narrows the umbilical artery, which decreases blood flow to the placenta.

- There is a 27 percent increased risk of death during or before birth in babies whose mothers smoked throughout pregnancy.

- Just as nicotine increases your heart rate, it does the same for your baby each time you puff a cigarette.

- The growth of the baby is limited including shorter stature, smaller head, and smaller arm circumferences.

- There is an increased risk of neurological damage to babies born to smoking mothers.

- There is an increased risk of both early rupture of your membrane and infections for smoking women.

- Infants born to smoking mothers have low birth weight. This does not mean that they are simply small and cute. Low birth weight can lead to multiple medical complications with long-lasting complications.

6

Smoking as a Habit

"A craving is a psychological itch.
Scratching only makes it worse.
Dwelling on it makes it unbearable.
The best thing to do is to acknowledge
the itch—then let it go and get on
with other things."

—Sandi Griffith

Are you smoking without being aware that you are smoking? How many times have you found yourself smoking a cigarette without remembering lighting up or getting a cigarette? Do you ever light up a cigarette but have one already burning in the ashtray? If you answered *yes* to any or all of these questions, you probably tell yourself and others that smoking is a *"habit,"* and that you can't help yourself.

It is important to understand how your smoking has developed into a habit and how you continue to maintain this habit. Then you can break away from the role of helpless victim to a *"habit."* Changing a habit requires awareness and active participation on your part. This chapter will help you get your smoking more under *your* control.

How does smoking *become* a habit in the first place? It happens as you begin to link smoking with all of your everyday activities, emotions, and situations. Keep in mind, smoking was not *always* linked with everything that you did. It's time to take a closer look at how your smoking habit began.

Thinking Back

Do you remember your first cigarette? In the space below, please describe what it was like to smoke your first cigarette: How old were you? Who were you with? Remember the physical sensations. Was it pleasant? Did you cough, or did your throat burn? Use as many details as you can to re-create the scene vividly.

Example:

I remember walking out of high school with Laura. It was sunny—the beginning of spring. She took out a pack and flipped it open, real casual and cool. Did I want one? I said "Sure." I remember putting it in my mouth, and she lit it. I inhaled right away and coughed. It burned! We both laughed, although I didn't think it was that funny. I tried again, and I remember feeling cool as we hung out near all the kids walking home. I kept trying not to choke.

Your Memory:

_____

_____

_____

_____

_____

Did one or both of your parents smoke? Other family friends? Friends?

_____

_____

_____

_____

Why and when did you smoke again? How do you remember feeling—cool? More grown up?

_____

_____

_____

_____

Describe how you see yourself as a smoker now—for example, more confident, rebellious, stylish, or fun? Consider negatives too, such as dependent, dirty, smelling of tobacco, etc.

_____   _____

_____

_____

_____

_____

_____

Typically, smokers report that they smoked their first cigarette during late childhood or during their teenage years. They either imitated a family member (after years of watching Dad or Mom smoke) or a friend encouraged them to try one. But many smokers also report that smoking their first cigarette was not a pleasant experience! You, too, may have coughed a lot, your eyes and throat burning. You may not have even known how to inhale! It certainly was not the same "pleasant" feeling you may experience now.

Building a Habit

You may have found yourself experimenting once or twice per week or month in spite of the first unpleasant experience because your friends smoked or it made you feel that you were older. You may have seen advertisements that picture smokers who are young, beautiful, and strong, and appear to have the world at their fingertips. Seeing your favorite actor or actress smoking might also have had a strong impact on your decision to see what cigarettes were all about, even though smoking that first one was unpleasant. Soon you may have lit up every time you went out with your friends. Slowly cigarettes became *linked* or associated in your mind with having a good time and relaxing (since most probably you were having fun with your friends). Therefore, having a good time or relaxing became a **cue** to smoke.

Soon you probably started to smoke at other times—in different situations or when you were feeling tense or bored. Smoking then becomes linked to a wider variety of situations, emotions, and people in your life. These links or associations become strengthened through thousands of repetitions (as your smoking increases to one to two packs per day, say, multiplied by several years). Situations, emotions, and people become **cues** or **triggers** to smoke a cigarette. For example, how often do you think of a cigarette with a cup of coffee? A cigarette when you start the car? A cigarette after you finish a meal and lean back in your chair? Or how about a cigarette after a hard day's work, or after an argument? By now for you, these activities probably seem to "fit" naturally together like salt and pepper, or peanut butter and jelly. Smoking fits with these activities because you have paired them together hundreds, maybe thousands of times. Therefore, drinking a cup of coffee, getting in the car, and leaning back in your chair after a meal serve as cues to get a cigarette. Reaching for a cigarette also becomes natural when you feel anxious, angry, or socially awkward.

The following exercises will help you further understand how these cues maintain your smoking habit, and how they have become part of your daily life without your being consciously aware of them.

You Smoke When . . .

Read the following scenarios and mark which ones apply to you.

___ 1. You have just finished your favorite dinner; you push your plate away and reach for a cigarette.

___ 2. You are waiting in the cashier's line at your local drugstore, you spot the cigarette stand with your favorite brand. You decide to buy a carton.

___ 3. You are under a lot of pressure at work to finish a project. You know the pressure will continue for a while. A cigarette might ease the pressure so that you may work better.

___ 4. You are waiting at a restaurant for a friend who is half an hour late. You have already ordered a drink. You think a cigarette would help pass the time.

___ 5. You have just picked up your car from the mechanic and the bill is much higher than you expected it to be. As you drive home, you find that the very problem you took the car in for is still not fixed and it stalls at a light. You feel angry and frustrated: you need a cigarette.

___ 6. You've had a stressful, hectic day at work—everybody needed something from you and it seemed as though you would never get caught up with your work. Finally, you get home but you are still tense from work. A cigarette would help relax you.

___ 7. You are at a party with friends. Others are smoking and drinking. You have a glass of wine in your hand and you are laughing and having fun. You always have a cigarette with a drink.

___ 8. You are on your way to a job interview and a traffic jam on the highway may makes you late. You start to feel anxious and a cigarette would calm your nerves.

___ 9. You are home alone with nothing to really do; nothing seems interesting—so you reach for a cigarette.

___ 10. You are sitting on your deck with some friends having a barbecue on a warm summer evening. You are relaxed and having a good time. One of your friends lights a cigarette which looks so refreshing to you.

Adapted from Shiffman et al., 1983, Smoking Situational Competency Test.

Personal High Risk Situations

Please mark which of the following situations you smoke in.

___ 1. I smoke when I feel frustrated about something or when things aren't going well.

___ 2. When I get angry at someone, I light up.

___ 3. When I finish eating, I almost always reach for a cigarette.

___ 4. My coffee always tastes better with a cigarette.

___ 5. I smoke to keep myself from gaining weight.

___ 6. When I am at a party or other social gatherings, I like to smoke to keep my hands busy.

___ 7. When I want to relax, a cigarette does the trick.

___ 8. When I wake up in the morning, one of the first things I do is smoke a cigarette.

___ 9. I usually smoke when I am waiting around or when I have nothing to do.

___ 10. When I feel happy or excited, I smoke a cigarette.

Why Smokers Smoke

Most smokers check almost all of the above scenarios or situations. You, too, probably smoke on most of these occasions. As stated before, feeling nervous, angry, or frustrated becomes a **trigger** to smoke in order to feel better. The above situations can be grouped into some common categories which serve as cues for most smokers to get a cigarette. These are listed below.

Eating and/or food substitution—smoking with drinking coffee or after meals. Also smoking to keep from eating too much and gaining weight.

Negative feelings—smoking when feeling angry, tense, worried, or frustrated; smoking seems to make bad feelings better.

Positive feelings—some smokers like to smoke when feeling good so that they will feel even better.

Boredom—smoking is something to do and the stimulating effects of nicotine help alleviate boredom.

Social—smoking helps combat any awkwardness in social situations by giving hands something to do; improves self-image (increases confidence because smoker believes they look more self-assured); also seeing other smokers serves as cue to smoke.

Alcohol—commonly associated with smoking.

While there may be other situations not described above in which you smoke, the following exercise can help you understand that almost everything that you do, feel, or experience every day has become associated with smoking—so much so that smoking is now an automatic habit. If you have tried to quit in the past and were successful for only a short period of time, it is not necessarily because your body needed the nicotine and you couldn't help yourself. Yes, it is true that you were physiologically addicted to nicotine. Each time that you inhaled you received a "hit" of nicotine, which means that nicotine was absorbed into your bloodstream. As you continued to smoke over time, your body "demanded" more of the nicotine. This is how the physical addiction strengthens the psychological addiction.

However, as you will learn in the subsequent chapters, nicotine will leave your body after only a few days. Your craving for cigarettes is not so much physical as it is psychological—your everyday life contains several cues and triggers reminding you to smoke. In your past attempts to quit, you may not have broken these automatic links. You will have more success in staying off cigarettes if you can first recognize the psychological part of your habit and then begin to break those links.

Identifying Your Smoking Pattern

This next exercise is an important one in helping you identify your own smoking patterns. Approaching quitting in a systematic manner will help make the whole process more manageable. Please look at the chart on page 50. This is what is referred to by behavior therapists as a self-monitoring form. The concept of self-monitoring simply involves keeping a daily record of your smoking habit. A self-record serves several purposes. First, it will give you a more objective picture of exactly how much you smoke. It will provide information about when you tend to smoke more. Identifying the situations in which you smoke will help you identify how you feel at the time (i.e., frustrated, bored). Continuing to monitor your own smoking will help you pinpoint "trouble spots" so that you can anticipate even before quitting when you are likely to really "need a cigarette." All this information will let you substitute an alternate coping strategy. Also, by monitoring your smoking, you make an unconscious act more conscious. That will help you eliminate those automatic and least important cigarettes from your routine.

Daily Smoking Record

Make at least ten copies of the Daily Smoking Record. Fold the first copy, and wrap it around your current pack of cigarettes. When you have the urge to smoke, take out the chart and follow the directions outlined below before you light the cigarette. If you think that's too time consuming, consider the time and energy that went into developing your habit in the first place. This time, your energy will be repaid healthfully.

On the far left corner, you'll see a column entitled "Cig. #." Just jot down the number, in order, of the cigarettes you smoke that day. For each cigarette that you smoke, check how you are feeling and the situation you are in. If the feelings listed do not accurately describe you own feelings at the time, feel free to fill in your own description. For example, the next cigarette that you smoke will be cigarette number 1. If you are at work, check the column marked "work"; if you are just finishing a meal then check the column marked "eating" or "drinking alcohol." Also, include with cigarette number 1 how you are feeling. For example, if you find yourself experiencing symptoms of anxiety check the column marked "nervous." If you find yourself feeling physically relaxed then check the column marked "relaxed." If none of these feelings or situations apply to you, add your own description under the column marked "other." Be sure to describe that "other" feeling or situation so that you'll recognize it later. As you can see, you may have several check marks in the row marked cigarette number 1. Now that you have identified what you're doing and what feeling you're experiencing, it is time to rate how important this cigarette is to you.

In the far right column of the chart, you will see a column marked, "How important is this cigarette?" This is your "need rating." The number 1 represents that this cigarette is most important to you, and number 4 indicates that this cigarette is being smoked out of habit and is not that important. If you rate the cigarette 1 or 2, indicating that you strongly feel the need to smoke the cigarette, go ahead and smoke it. If you rated the cigarette 3 or 4, indicating that you probably could do without this cigarette, *even for a while*, hold off on smoking it. Put some time between this cigarette and your next one.

Do this for each cigarette that you smoke now until your quit date. And remember, if you have time to smoke your cigarette, you have time to fill in the chart. No excuses.

After one to two weeks of filling in the charts, you will begin to see your pattern of smoking emerge. For example, you may tend to smoke more when you are at work or more when you feel depressed. These times and feeling states become your "high risk" areas that will need to be addressed before quitting. You will also notice that by merely keeping track of your cigarettes and eliminating the least important ones (i.e., 3's and 4's), you will automatically cut down on your smoking. You will need to refer back to these charts in the following chapters when discussing your personal "high risk" areas and alternative coping strategies. Keep at it.

Daily Smoking Record

Cig. #	SITUATION/PLACE					ACTIVITY					FEELING							HOW IMPORTANT IS THIS CIGARETTE?
	WORK	HOME	CAR	BAR	OTHER (WHERE?)	EATING	WATCHING TV	DRINKING COFFEE	DRINKING ALCOHOL	OTHER (WHAT?)	ANGRY	BORED	DEPRESSED	SAD	NERVOUS	RELAXED	OTHER (HOW?)	VERY IMPORTANT 1 — SMOKE THE CIGARETTE 2 CAN DO WITHOUT THIS CIGARETTE 3 4 — DO NOT SMOKE THE CIGARETTE

II

ALTERNATIVE COPING
TECHNIQUES AND STRATEGIES

7

Anxiety

This chapter and subsequent chapters were designed to provide you with healthy alternative coping strategies to use instead of reaching for a cigarette. In chapter 6 you identified your own personal "high risk" situations. Some of the chapters that follow may or may not apply to you. Proceed by locating the high risk areas that do apply to you and following the healthy alternatives.

You may currently be using cigarettes to manage symptoms of anxiety as well as situational stressors. It's time to consider how various anxiety triggers may be related to your smoking habit, and to explore healthy alternative techniques to cope with each.

Symptoms of Anxiety Related to Nicotine Withdrawal

As a smoker you may have experienced feelings of jitteriness, tension, and nervousness when time has passed without a cigarette. These symptoms may make you feel like you are "climbing the walls," are less tolerant, "crabby," and difficult to deal with (or so you may have been told by others). These symptoms or feelings may be part of nicotine withdrawal which is your body's way of requesting more of the drug, nicotine. When you smoke your cigarette in response to these symptoms you *reinforce* your smoking as a way to manage these negative feelings. The next time you experience these symptoms of anxiety you will *automatically* reach for a cigarette because you know that it worked in the past. There are two main problems with this behavior. First, you keep the cycle of addiction going by physically reinforcing the addiction. Second, you begin to give credit to your cigarette instead of to yourself for being able to cope effectively with anxiety-producing events. This serves to undermine your natural ability to cope with anxiety in a more healthy way.

The good news is you can break this behavior/thought cycle. You'll want to interrupt the flow of associations telling you that smoking is the only way to calm yourself. Practice

Managing Symptoms of Anxiety Related to Nicotine Withdrawal

1. Remind yourself that the symptoms of anxiety that you are experiencing are caused by the physical withdrawal process from nicotine.

2. Tell yourself that this is your body's way of healing itself. The discomfort you are feeling will lead to overall healing and improved health. It is "good" pain.

3. Remind yourself that these symptoms of anxiety will last for only a couple of weeks. The worst feeling will be around the third or fourth day after your last cigarette.

4. Practice visualizing how nicotine acts on your nervous system by increasing your heart rate and blood pressure. Next visualize how *without* nicotine your heart rate and blood pressure will return to normal. This, in turn, will help you feel more relaxed.

5. You may want to picture your anxiety as a wave. You can feel it rise—but as you ride it out you can feel it subside. It passes without any action on your part.

the simple steps above. Each wave of anxiety you ride out successfully, without reaching for a cigarette, will prove to you that you *can* relax without smoking, even if only for the moment. You'll reinforce non-smoking behavior, and meanwhile time will pass breaking your physical craving for nicotine. It only takes a few days to move past the strongest desire.

Stressors

You may have recognized that certain situations, people, and events can cause you to experience various levels of anxiety. Sometimes you're aware of your stressors, and sometimes they're hard to pinpoint. In the past, chances are you coped with this anxiety by automatically reaching for a cigarette. The first step in developing more healthy and adaptive responses involves identifying what thoughts, feelings, and cues in your environment contribute to your feeling anxious.

You may experience anxiety as a jittery feeling, or as overall muscle tension. It is through understanding and being aware of these cues, such as feelings of tension, social discomfort, feelings of inadequacy, and your *interpretation* of these feelings and events, that you can best manage anxiety. For example, a red stop light signals you to automatically stop your vehicle. When you see the red signal you automatically, without thought, respond by placing your foot on the brake. Similarly, you may automatically be responding to cues that evoke anxiety without consciously thinking about them. In the past, you would probably react by reaching for a cigarette to manage this feeling of anxiety without consciously being aware of it, or by *telling* yourself that a cigarette would calm you.

Identifying Your Anxiety Signals

When a stressful situation occurs, how you cope or don't cope with the event may depend on your interpretation of the situation. This exercise will help make you more aware of your own personal "signals" and interpretations of anxiety. It will also reveal how you can manage them more effectively *without* cigarettes. Take a few minutes to think about the last time you experienced great anxiety. Try to identify as many "signals" or cues as you can that made you feel uncomfortable. It will help to visualize the situation, and to write about it in the present tense. Pay attention to all the things of which you are aware, including sights, smells, sounds, feelings, and thoughts. Take a few minutes to write about this anxiety-producing experience as vividly as you can. (If you like, make several blank copies of this form before you write in it. Write records of several situations so that you have ample data to draw from.)

Example:

Situation: *Giving a presentation before an audience.*

What happened just before the anxious situation (people encountered, thoughts remembered, etc.): *Ran into several co-workers who said, "Looking forward to hearing what you have to say." Remembered that the last presentation did not go as smoothly as I wanted.*

Sights, sounds, smells of the situation: *People beginning to take their seats; the room is buzzing with people talking; the temperature of the room feels warm.*

Physical signals of discomfort (knot in stomach, sweaty palms, etc.): *Palms are sweaty, heart racing, knot in stomach, dry mouth.*

Thoughts: *I am going to stutter; I am going to go blank and not be able to speak; people will be bored; I'll look like I don't know what I'm talking about.*

Feelings: *I feel nervous and scared.*

Situation: _____

_____

_____

_____

_____

What happened just before the anxious situation (people encountered, thoughts remembered, etc.): _____

_____

_____

Sights, sounds, smells of the situation: _____

_____

_____

Physical signals of discomfort (knot in stomach, sweaty palms, etc.): _____

_____

_____

_____

Thoughts: _____

_____

_____

_____

Feelings: _____

_____

_____

Now it's time to comb your recollections for their essential information. From the experience(s) you described, briefly make a note of each "signal" you identified here in the lefthand column of the Anxiety Log on page 58. This might be a meeting with a difficult person, a stressful time of day, a remembered obligation—whatever you found yourself doing when the feeling of anxiety first hit. Next, try to isolate the stressful thought. This goes in the second column, marked "Negative Thought." Maybe you told yourself you were "in trouble now," or maybe you thought "I'm not good enough to make this work out right." Just write down an approximation of the words you told yourself. Next, in the third column (marked "Feeling"), try to define the core feeling behind the thought. Examples include fear, shame, despair, anger, guilt, sadness—or maybe even something hopeful that felt let down. Finally, in the righthand column, try to change your negative thoughts about the situation to more positive and realistic thoughts. You might respond to the feeling; for instance, if you wrote "despair," you could write, "There is always reason for hope. Things are always changing, and are likely to get better." Or you can respond to the thought. If you wrote "I'm no good at this job," write "I'm good at many parts of this job, including x, y, and z. I'm getting better at this part, too." Take time to write accurate coping statements *now*, since you'll want to have them ready when anxiety strikes.

Before moving on to the rest of this chapter, see what other useful information you can gather from the anxiety signals you identified. Did you notice your physical cues, such as racing heart, sudden sweating, or worried glances at your watch? Try to identify your particular signs of anxiety, so you can turn to coping techniques before the anxiety builds—and before you reach for a cigarette.

Physical Anxiety Signals

_____

_____

You may also have noticed situational cues. Perhaps a particular time of day sparks your anxiety, or seeing a particular person. Maybe every time you think of your mother you reach for a cigarette, before you even realize the lightning fast chain of associations leading you from situation to negative thought to negative feeling to coping mechanism. Look for anxious situations you can predict, and list them below. Sights, smells, and sounds belong here as well.

Situational Cues

_____

_____

The rest of this chapter will offer alternative coping strategies to help you cut through your most anxious moments. Additional exercises follow in chapters 8, 9, and 10 on Social Discomfort, Stress, and Depression. Keep working on these records until you have an accurate sense of when *you* need to be on your guard against the pressures of anxiety.

Relaxation Training

Relaxation training is a process that helps people improve their ability to focus their attention on their bodies. Relaxation methods will enable you to effectively reduce both your mental anxiety, and its physical signs. As you become more relaxed, you may be able to listen better to important things you want to say to yourself. These may be general thoughts, or thoughts

Anxiety Log

	Situation	Negative Thought	Feeling	Coping Statement
Ex.	I'm fighting with Bill about dinner	This marriage doesn't work	Despair	Many parts of this marriage are great. We've worked through so much, we can work this out too.
	_____	_____	_____	_____
	_____	_____	_____	_____
	_____	_____	_____	_____
	_____	_____	_____	_____
	_____	_____	_____	_____
	_____	_____	_____	_____
	_____	_____	_____	_____
	_____	_____	_____	_____
	_____	_____	_____	_____
	_____	_____	_____	_____
	_____	_____	_____	_____
	_____	_____	_____	_____
	_____	_____	_____	_____

specifically related to your smoking. Relaxation training is a self-control technique, where *you* are in control of your level of relaxation. Like any skill, the more you practice the better able you will become to relax more fully and in less ideal situations.

Sometimes people wonder if they can get so good at relaxation that they won't be able to respond when they need to. This is impossible. Once you are in a relaxed state you can choose to respond when you want to. For example, if the phone rings or an interruption occurs, you can attend to it immediately if you *choose* to do so. But you can also choose to tune out unwanted stressors.

Keep in mind that in relaxation training you can control how relaxed you get. The following is an example of how relaxation training works. The more vividly you try to imagine this scene, the more relaxation you will experience.

Relaxation and Breathing Practice

To begin the exercise find a comfortable chair in a quiet room. Now concentrate on your breathing, taking slow deep breaths. Breathe through your nose, inhale, hold it, exhale slowly. Focus on your belly as it expands like a balloon when you inhale and deflates when you exhale. Allow your belly to expand, and then your chest as you fill your lungs with good, clean air. Then let your belly deflate fully, followed by your chest as you blow out all tension from your body. Pause, and repeat this deep breathing for several minutes. Aim for a slow, comfortable rhythm.

As you concentrate on slowing down your breathing, also slow down your thinking. Let your body sink into your comfortable chair. Notice how relaxed your arms feel against the chair. So do your legs, your back, and your neck. Notice that your breathing is slow, deep, and regular. Continue to imagine that you are inhaling fresh, clean air into your lungs, which are able to expand more fully when you are not smoking. Imagine each breath as a cleansing breath, helping your body to heal itself. As you exhale, imagine that you are releasing every last bit of tension from your body. You are becoming more relaxed. Notice how the clean air enters your body more fully. Your arms and your legs become warm and heavy. Your neck and your back begin to feel more relaxed. The tension slowly begins to fade each time that you exhale. Your body is cleaning and healing itself.

Deep Breathing and Visualization

If you like, you can combine the breathing exercise above with a visualization for deeper overall relaxation. Read through this scene before you try to immerse yourself in it. You may want to remember a version of it, or to tape record it so that you can relax with your eyes closed. You might simply choose to create a scene of your own, once you get the idea. Remember to keep the details vivid.

As you relax, imagine this scene. You are going for a walk in the woods on a beautiful fall day. Imagine entering a forest path. Feel the cool shade of many trees. As you walk slowly down the path, notice the trees, underbrush, and fallen branches. Perhaps there is a slightly damp smell of fresh earth and fallen leaves, or the deep fragrance of pine. You may hear the crunch of dry leaves under your feet, or the rustle of a small friendly animal. Now and then, a bird calls overhead, and you look up to see it gently soaring, sailing skyward. Perhaps you reach over and pick up a stick or a colored leaf, and carry it with you. As you walk on, another pleasant sound begins, at first faintly in the distance, then louder, the clear sound of rushing water. As you walk on, a clearing appears. You step into the clearing, and notice that the sun feels warm on your face. A slight breeze gently blows your hair. You notice the sun sparkling on the water of a clear stream. You hear it gurgling as it rushes over rocks. As you walk toward the stream, you notice a large log lying on the bank, a perfect spot to rest and look at the stream. You may want to sit down for a few minutes. Looking in the water, you may see small fish swimming lazily, like colored rocks on the bottom of the beautiful stream. You notice how relaxed your body feels.

As you look in the water, feeling more relaxed than you have in a long time, you may feel like taking a few moments to tell yourself some things that are important to you. After all, you are finally relaxed and better able to listen to yourself with respect and full attention. You may say general things to yourself, or you may tailor your observations to cope with a stressful situation. For example,

"I am in control of my reaction in this situation."

"I will manage those things that I have control over and let go of those that I can't control."

"What evidence do I have for thinking this way?"

If you are using relaxation to manage your craving for a cigarette you may say things to yourself that will help you manage the desire. For example,

"I am able to inhale more deeply without cigarettes."

"Each day without cigarettes my body continues to heal."

"This urge or desire is only temporary and will only last for a few seconds."

"I am able to achieve deeper, fuller relaxation without cigarettes."

Pause for several minutes while you repeat these important thoughts to yourself.

Notice how much more relaxed and comfortable you may have become and how much you've enjoyed being in this place. Focus on how relaxed your arms, legs, back, and neck feel. In a few minutes you are going to bring yourself back by slowing down your breathing. You know that when you want you can bring yourself back to this spot.

Now begin slowing down your breathing while retracing your steps down the path. When you are ready, count backwards from five to one. When you reach one, you will open your eyes, feeling relaxed, refreshed, alert, and ready to do what you want to do.

Begin practicing these relaxation exercises twice a week for 30 minutes. If the example used here of walking in the woods is not particularly relaxing to you, then substitute a day at the beach or some other place that you have been that was particularly peaceful. The key to effective relaxation exercises is to make the imagery as vivid and real as you can. Therefore, when you are imagining this scene or your own scene it is important to try to imagine as many sights, smells, feelings, and sounds as you can. Try to place yourself into the scene in such a way that you can feel the breeze or the sun, and hear the waves, the birds, etc.

Try practicing these exercises on a regular basis so that you become very good at relaxing deeply and quickly. As with any skill, with time and practice you will improve. Your goal is to benefit from these exercises at any time, including your most stressful when you are craving a cigarette.

8

Social Discomfort

Jane arrived at a party which she had been looking forward to all week. However, when she entered the room she began to feel awkward. She noticed her face beginning to flush, her heart beginning to beat faster, and her palms starting to sweat. Subsequently, she began saying to herself, "I'm not dressed properly," "Anything I say will probably sound stupid," etc. With each thought she began to feel more uncomfortable and judged by others at the party. As the discomfort increased, she found herself reaching for a cigarette. With the cigarette in her hand she felt more relaxed, suddenly feeling that she fit in with the crowd better. With the cigarette to occupy her hands she felt less socially awkward.

How similar to Jane are you?

Assessment of Social Interactions

Think about how you typically react in a social situation. Answer each of the questions below by circling the number which most describes your reactions.

A. Your Body Reactions

	Hardly Ever		Very Often	
1. Does your heart race?	1	2	3	4
2. Do you perspire?	1	2	3	4
3. Do you experience butterflies in your stomach?	1	2	3	4
4. Does your face flush?	1	2	3	4
5. Do you twist your hands?	1	2	3	4

Listed below are several statements that people make to themselves during social situations. Circle the number which most applies to your own thoughts when in a social situation.

B. Self-Statements

	Hardly Ever		Very Often	
1. I will probably sound stupid if I voice my opinion.	1	2	3	4
2. Everyone will notice how physically uncomfortable I am.	1	2	3	4
3. Nobody will want to talk to me.	1	2	3	4
4. I feel people are critical.	1	2	3	4
5. I won't be able to make eye contact with people.	1	2	3	4

If you tend to feel uncomfortable in social situations you probably either avoid the situations which keep the discomfort going, or you attempt to cope with the situation by using cigarettes. Listed below are a number of behaviors that people will frequently engage in when they are uncomfortable in a social situation. Circle the number that most applies to you.

C. Behaviors in a Social Situation

	Hardly Ever		Very Often	
1. I busy myself with lighting and smoking a cigarette.	1	2	3	4
2. I offer to help serve food or assist with activities to avoid people.	1	2	3	4
3. I fidget and or pace around the room.	1	2	3	4
4. I avoid making eye contact.	1	2	3	4
5. I usually agree with what everyone is saying.	1	2	3	4

If you circled a 3 or a 4 for most of the statements, you probably tend to feel rather uncomfortable in social situations. The things that you say to yourself, how you focus on your physical symptoms, and your behaviors all play an important role in your ability to cope effectively with social discomfort.

Body Reactions

It is almost impossible to change either the statements that you make to yourself or your behavior when you are in a high state of physical tension. Therefore, the first step in dealing with social discomfort is to control your physical tension. Once you reduce the physical tension you will notice that you can concentrate better, have more energy, and feel more motivated to make other changes.

You can use any technique or combination of techniques that relax you including the imagery and relaxation exercises used in the previous chapter, on anxiety. Other effective techniques include physical exercise, hot baths, or even chores around the house. Several specific techniques have been recommended for dealing with the physical arousal that is associated with social discomfort. Both diaphragmatic breathing and progressive muscle relaxation help cut through the physiological arousal associated with social discomfort. These techniques will be described in this section.

Diaphragmatic Breathing

This technique involves breathing from your diaphragm instead of your chest. Your diaphragm is a muscle that is located just below your ribs. Breathing from the diaphragm involves slow deep breaths where the diaphragm actually pulls and pushes air in and out of the lungs. Breathing from the diaphragm promotes relaxation in the body, as opposed to the shallow, rapid, and tense breathing that occurs in the chest when you are anxious.

Learning to breathe from your diaphragm brings you many physical benefits. First, this type of breathing makes relaxation on a physical level much easier to achieve. Second, this type of breathing is physically more efficient and subsequently increases the oxygen supply to the brain and other organs. This is particularly important for smokers who already have a reduction of oxygen to the brain due to the effects of nicotine. Also, diaphragmatic breathing more efficiently gets rid of toxins from the body. Again, this is particularly important to you as a smoker because after you quit smoking your body will begin to heal, and part of the healing process is the removal of toxins from the body. By using this type of breathing you make the healing process smoother and more complete.

1. Place your hand on your abdomen below your rib cage. This is where your diaphragm is located.

2. Take in a deep breath through your nose and then slowly exhale. You should be able to feel your stomach moving out when you inhale and in when you exhale.

3. Repeat several deep breaths. After you inhale hesitate for a moment and then slowly exhale.

4. Remember to inhale *slowly* but deeply, and to exhale slowly but *evenly*.

5. Avoid rapid, quick breaths. Hyperventilation tends to increase tension throughout your body.

6. You may wish to combine imagery and positive self-statements with the breathing exercise. For example, when you exhale imagine letting all of the tension in your body go with the breath. You may also imagine all of the toxins from your cigarette smoke leaving your body with each exhalation. You may imagine that when you inhale you are better able to take air in more fully as a non-smoker.

Progressive Muscle Relaxation

Progressive muscle relaxation was developed by Dr. Jacobson over fifty years ago. He found that you could achieve great relaxation in your muscles by first *tensing* them. When you are working on tensing a particular muscle group you need to try to keep all other muscle groups relaxed.

1. Begin by getting yourself in a quiet and comfortable position.

2. Take several deep cleansing breaths from the diaphragm.

3. When you tense a muscle group you need to do so in an intense manner, holding it for 7–10 seconds.

4. Release the tension from the muscle group in an abrupt way. You will feel a relaxed sensation. Enjoy the relaxation for 15–20 seconds.

5. Make a tight fist. Hold it (7–10 seconds) and the release it (15–20 seconds).

6. Tense the muscles around your eyes by tightly holding your eyelids closed. Hold it, and release.

7. Open your mouth as widely as you can. Hold it and then release.

8. Raise your eyebrow as high as you can, tensing your forehead. Hold it and then release.

9. Make a "muscle" and tense your biceps. Hold it and then release.

10. Stiffen your arms and extend to them to your side and tense your triceps. Hold it and then release.

11. "Shrug" your shoulders by raising them up to your ears. Hold it and then release.

12. Pull your shoulder blades back as if you were sticking out your chest. Hold it and then release it.

13. Suck in your stomach. Hold it and then release.

14. Arch your lower back. Hold it and then release.

15. "Pinch" the muscles of your buttocks together. Hold it and then release.

16. Pull your toes up toward you and tighten your calf muscles in your legs. Hold it and then release.

17. Curl your toes down towards the floor. Hold it and then release.

Initially, the above exercise may take you 20 to 30 minutes to complete. With practice you will be able to reduce the time and will be able to achieve relaxation even in less ideal situations. You will need to practice progressive muscle relaxation in a quiet relaxed atmosphere before you can learn to do this exercise under stressful situations. Remember, you can also use this exercise in combination with other relaxation activities already discussed.

Rewriting Your Self-Statements

Your thoughts about a situation can lead to an increase in anxiety. What you *say* to yourself about how you handle yourself in social situations can lead you to feel that you are uncomfortable and nervous, and therefore need a cigarette. In the section above you were asked to rate how a few self-statements apply to you. Below is a list of those statements plus others. Identify which of the statements apply to you and write a persuasive counterargument for the statement.

Self-Statement	*Counterargument*
"I will probably sound stupid if I voice my opinion."	*"I am confident in my opinions and my right to state them."*
"Everyone will notice how physically uncomfortable I am."	*"Although I feel uncomfortable inside, chances are that others will not notice my hands sweating and my heart pounding."*
"Nobody will want to talk to me."	*"I have been in similar situations before and people have talked to me."*
"I feel people are critical."	_____
"I am not attractive enough."	_____
"I can't talk to strangers."	_____
"My voice will shake and everyone will know I'm nervous."	_____
"I'm not funny enough."	_____
"I am not outgoing."	_____
"I find it hard to join conversations."	_____
"I worry about what others will think of me."	_____

Self-Statement	*Counterargument*
"I don't feel comfortable going places alone."	_____
"Without a cigarette I won't know what to do with my hands."	_____
"I need a cigarette to feel sophisticated."	_____

What other kinds of statements do you make to yourself?

_____

_____

_____

When you look at the list of things that you say to yourself, do you notice any themes?

_____

_____

For example, are your self-statements usually about feeling judged by others? Not having confidence in yourself? Worrying about your appearance or your conversation? List your themes.

_____

_____

_____

Go back to each of your self-statements and write an alternative counterargument for each statement. When you are writing your statements make them specific. Ask what evidence you have for each negative statement. Keep your counterargument focused in the present.

Behavior

Learning Social Skills

Frequently people may experience discomfort in social situations because they do not feel equipped with skills to interact with others. Doubting your skills and your ability to *handle* yourself in a social situation only serves to make you feel more self-conscious. This vicious cycle deepens feelings of social discomfort.

There are many skills involved in interacting with people in general and specifically in social situations. Here are five important skills that may help you feel more at ease when interacting with others.

1. Ability to read non-verbal cues. Part of the discomfort that people experience in social situations is often a result of their misinterpretation of others' body language. Have you ever said to yourself, "they *look* bored when I am talking," or "they seem like they are evaluating me"? These statements can stem from over-interpretations or misperceptions of body language. For example, people may yawn or not make great eye contact with you because they are lacking sleep or because they themselves are uncomfortable in social situations, and not because they find you boring. It is important to not base all of your interpretations on body language alone. It is also important that you pay attention to your own body language. Perhaps you are not aware of all the signals you send to others. For example, you may physically separate yourself from others by standing apart. Or perhaps you tend to make poor eye contact with others, or you cross your arms in front of you as a way to keep your distance. Such unconscious behaviors may be feeding into your own sense of isolation, discomfort, and even rejection by the group. Reading others' non-verbal cues and recognizing your own is a skill that takes practice.

Exercise. Get together with a friend or a family member that you trust. Ask the other person to observe your non-verbal cues at some upcoming function, and then have them give you feedback on what they observe. Likewise reverse roles and provide that person with feedback on what you observe.

What did the other person tell you about your non-verbal cues?

_____

_____

_____

Work on noticing these behaviors in yourself, if they're accurate. Then see how far you can progress in letting some barriers down.

2. Develop active listening skills. Good listening skills will help you interact more completely with others, which will in turn make you feel more comfortable in social situations. Although most people believe that they are good listeners, they usually are not. Listening is a skill that like any other skill requires *practice*. To be a good listener means more than just hearing what the other person is saying. It means fully understanding the content of what the other person is saying—and registering that you hear and understand—in a non-judgmental way.

Here are some ways to improve your listening skills:

- *Avoid being judgmental and evaluative when listening to others.*

- *Avoid planning your next response while the other person is still talking.* If you are thinking about how to respond, you are probably not listening very well.

- *Avoid assuming that you know what the other person is saying.* Once you start assuming you understand, you stop listening to the content.

- *Repeat back to the other person what you just heard and understood in your own words.* Don't repeat verbatim like a parrot, but rather summarize the essence of what you heard. For example,

Joe: My boss gave me another assignment to complete while Stan appears to have time on his hands.

Response: You seem irritated at what seems to be unequal work assignments.

Joe: I'm not just irritated, I'm angry at the unequal treatment.

In order to repeat what you have heard, you need to pay close attention to what is being said to you. In other words, practice *active listening*. Moreover, by repeating back to the other person the essence of what you have heard, you give them the opportunity to clarify any misunderstandings. In the example above the response was correct that Joe did not like that there were unequal work assignments. However, the listener thought he was merely irritated by the situation but in reality he was angry. By repeating back to the speaker what you understood you give them the chance to explain their position more fully. This helps you the listener to understand more accurately and fully what is being conveyed to you. It also helps a speaker feel heard and validated.

3. Initiating and maintaining conversation. It may be difficult for you to go up to someone and just start a conversation. You may feel awkward and not sure where to begin. An easy rule of thumb to follow is to start conversations with open-ended questions. These are questions that cannot be answered with a simple yes or no answer. If you ask closed questions or questions that can be answered with a yes or no response you may end the discussion. That is, after the other person has responded the dialogue is limited. Open questions are those that ask what, when, where, and how. Avoid overusing "why" questions, as this can put people on the spot or make them feel defensive. Below is an example of conversation using first closed and then open questions.

Closed Questions

Jack: Do you like red wine?

Sue: Yes.

Open Questions

Jack: What kind of wine do you like?

Sue: I usually like red wine but on certain occasions I drink white.

Jack: They serve an excellent white wine here.

Sue: How do you know so much about wine?

Jack: I took a wine tasting class.

You can see from this example that conversation flowed with greater ease following the open-ended question. It provided the opportunity for more dialogue and interaction between the two people.

Make a list of open-ended questions that you could use in your next social interaction.

---

4. Asserting your needs, feelings, and opinions. Feeling socially awkward can stem from the belief that you have nothing to contribute to a conversation. Have you ever felt that others' opinions and views were better or more interesting than your own? Asserting your opinions, thoughts, and feelings will make you feel more confident in yourself. This in turn will be reflected in the way that you handle yourself in social situations.

Try these steps to improve your assertiveness.

1. *Keep in mind that assertiveness is not aggressiveness.* Assertiveness is a balance between the two extremes of aggressiveness and submissiveness. People who act in an aggressive style demand and expect others to do exactly what they want. Those who act in a submissive style give up their own beliefs, opinions, and wants to those of others. They feel guilty asking for what they want, as if others' needs were more important than their own. An assertive person respects others' views and feelings, but also values and respects his or her own.

2. *Look others directly in the eyes when talking to them and maintain an open posture.* This will be easier to do if you reinforce for yourself that what you are saying is important. Don't assume a posture that says you are apologizing for what you are saying. That's the message when, for example, you look at the ground or quickly away from others when speaking, when you add an inflection at the end of your statements as if questioning or doubting your own words, or when you speak in a timid voice.

3. *Be specific when making requests.* Vague requests or comments can often be misinterpreted by others or simply ignored. If your request is very specific and direct there is little room for confusion. For example, instead of asking for someone's help in general, specifically state with *what* you want help *when* and for *how* long.

4. *When discussing an opinion or making a request, use statements that begin with I.* For example, say I feel..., I want..., or I think.... When you use such "I-statements" it is more likely that others will be receptive to hearing what you have to say. Statements that start out with "you," such as, you said... or you think..., tend to put the other person on the defensive. He or she becomes less likely to be open to what you are saying.

5. *Observe the behavior, non-verbal cues, and conversations of others who appear to be comfortable in social situations.* Examine how your non-verbal cues, behavior, and conversation are similar and different from their style.

Name a few people who you have noticed seem at ease in social situations.

_____

_____

Which of their characteristics gives you the impression that they are at ease in social situations? Take some time to observe them, if you like.

_____

_____

_____

What similarities do you notice between your style in social situations and their style?

_____

_____

_____

What differences do you notice between their style and yours?

_____

_____

_____

Practice modeling the characteristics that you feel help them in social situations. For example, if they seem to assume a certain body posture, practice that posture when you are alone. Then try it when you are in a social situation.

Desensitization

Continuing to avoid social situations or relying on cigarettes as a crutch to help you cope with the situation will only continue to make your discomfort worse. One particular technique that you can use to break the association between relying on cigarettes and coping with periods of social discomfort is called *desensitization*. This process involves the use of imagery, real life social situations, and relaxation techniques to break the association.

Desensitization works progressively as you imagine and then confront a series of situations that range from not very anxiety-producing to extremely anxiety-producing. Anxiety-producing simply means that you feel social discomfort. You start by imagining the least anxiety-producing situation while you are doing relaxation exercises. The goal is for you to associate relaxation with the image or situation that used to spark anxiety or discomfort. After you are able to fully relax with an image of the *least* anxiety-producing situation, you then move on to an image of a more anxiety-producing situation and repeat the relaxation. This continues until you can imagine the most anxiety-producing situation while remaining calm. You may choose to confront each situation once you've conquered it imaginatively. Or you may prefer to imagine the whole series progressively, and then to return to the beginning in real-life situations.

Below is a hierarchy of situations that range from least anxiety-producing to most anxiety-producing. With each step imagine the scene as vividly as you can. Pay attention to signs in your body and in your thoughts that you are becoming uncomfortable and/or anxious. When you begin to feel the discomfort practice your favorite relaxation exercises. You may choose deep breathing, progressive muscle relaxation, or any other technique from chapters 7 and 8. When you can manage the scene without anxiety then move on to the next scene.

Try imagining these scenes:

1. Making plans to go to a party with a friend and leaving your cigarettes at home.

2. Going to a party with a friend and talking to one new person with your friend for a few minutes without a cigarette.

3. Going to a party with a friend and talking to one new person alone for a few minutes without a cigarette.

4. Going to a party with a friend and joining in the conversation of a group of three or four people alone for a few minutes without a cigarette.

5. Going to a party alone and joining in the conversation of a group of four or five people alone without a cigarette, and remaining in conversation for ten to fifteen minutes.

6. Going to a party alone and joining in the conversation of a large group of people without a cigarette, and remaining in conversation until the group breaks up.

Practice imagining these scenes for several weeks or months—whatever it takes for you to progress to the most anxiety-producing scene without discomfort. After you have been able to successfully imagine each of these scenes *in your mind* and have been able to remain calm and confident without cigarettes, then practice the *actual* scenes in real life. Feel free to adapt the scenes to your particular anxieties. The more the situation scares you now, the better prepared you will be to confront *all* similar anxiety-producing situations in a life free of cigarettes.

9

Stress

Many smokers say that they smoke because they have so much stress in their lives and cigarettes help them handle "their stress." But as you are discovering in this book, using cigarettes to manage any part of your life has long-term consequences to your health. Thus, it will be helpful to learn how to deal with stressors in your life without cigarettes.

What are your symptoms of stress? How do you know when you are experiencing stress? Generally, stress is a complex response, both physical and psychological, to some sort of demand from the environment. When the demands of the environment exceed your ability to cope, you may experience a more severe stress reaction. Smokers tend to use cigarettes to handle everyday demands as well as during times of greater stress.

Below is a list of symptoms that can be related to stress. Check the ones you have experienced or continue to experience.

irritability	headaches
difficulty with sleep	upset stomach
fatigue	poor concentration
appetite disturbance	teeth grinding
pounding heart	allergic skin reactions
muscle tension	decreased interest in sex
irritable bowel	unwanted thoughts
high blood pressure	low motivation
mood swings	withdrawn from others
angry outbursts	crying more than usual
nightmares	anxious, worrying

Some of these symptoms can be caused by medical problems. It is important if you are experiencing any of the physical symptoms in particular, to have them investigated by your physician. If medical causes have been ruled out, then these symptoms may be related to stress reactions. The more symptoms you checked above, the greater the stress you may be experiencing at this time. If symptoms of stress begin interfering with your daily functioning, you may want to consider seeking some professional assistance.

Prolonged functioning at a level of severe stress can decrease your body's ability to resist disease. The human body reacts to stress in various stages. During the initial phase, when you are first exposed to a stressor, your body responds automatically by releasing adrenaline for a "fight or flight response." You may experience this as feeling tense and more alert about what is going on. You may feel your heart begin to race, your palms sweat, and your breathing become shallow and rapid. Usually, smokers increase their smoking at this time in an effort to "calm down."

During the next phase, "resistance," the body continues to maintain a state of readiness. Hormones are released to help increase the level of blood sugar needed by the body to maintain this emergency state. However, these hormones interfere with the body's ability to resist disease. If the stressor continues, your body begins to wear down and you may become exhausted. This is the final stage, "exhaustion." It is at this time that you may experience more severe symptoms which make daily functioning difficult. It will be important to intervene before you reach this stage. Take the time now to learn effective anti-stress strategies before you even enter the second phase of resistance.

Stressors

There are plenty of situations and events in life, pleasant or unpleasant, that can cause stress in your life. Look at the list below. Have some of these occurred in your life?

death of a loved one	buying a home
newly married	selling a home
divorce or separation	moving to a new city
new baby	legal problems
illness or injury	financial problems
illness of loved one	graduating from school
starting new job	unpleasant work environment
losing job	difficult boss
retirement	demanding job
arguing with significant other	being a single parent
problems with children	victim of abuse or crime

Other stressors: _____

_____

Your everyday life is full of minor irritations which when accumulated over time can be stressful. These irritants can be things like driving in rush hour traffic or waiting in a long line at the supermarket. Having to manage household chores along with a career can also be stressful. Make a list of daily events that irritate you or cause you stress:

Daily Stressors

Examples: *Cooking dinner every night*
     Dealing with boss
     Being late for an appointment

Your Stressors: _____

_____

_____

_____

_____

As you can see, there are many different types of stressors. What is stressful for one person may not be stressful for you. Stressors can often feel unpredictable and out of your control. While this is true of many things that happen in your life, you *can* control how you deal with these stressors. Look over the stressors in your life that you checked above. Can any changes be made to avoid or lessen their impact? If so, what?

Brainstorming Solutions

Stressor   *Changes possible?*

Example: *Cooking dinner every night*   *Agree to go out more often, or convince*
                   spouse or a friend to share cooking duties,
                   or cook on Sunday for whole week. Or, try
                   to see if I can think of cooking time as private
                   time for reflection.

_____   _____

_____   _____

_____   _____

Stressor   *Changes possible?*

_____   _____

_____   _____

_____   _____

_____   _____

_____   _____

_____   _____

If you are like many people, you may have a short list. It is not uncommon to feel that all the stressors in your life are out of your control and that there is nothing you can do to change things. Donald Meichenbaum has developed a technique for handling stressors called "stress inoculation." There are four parts to this training: education, coping self-talk, relaxation, and practice.

1. Educate yourself about the stressor. If you don't have information about the stressor, it is difficult to make decisions about a course of action. A lack of knowledge contributes to feeling helpless. For instance, if you have an illness but don't know much about it and possible treatments, you may feel confused and upset. So find out as much as you can about the stressor from other people, including professionals and books. You may find out how others have coped in similar situations.

2. Talk to yourself with positive coping statements. Talking to yourself *positively* is a powerful way of increasing your ability to cope. Many people talk to themselves in a negative manner, making statements like "I can't deal with this." This is exactly the time when you probably reach for a cigarette. Substitute this negative message with a positive one like, "I *can* handle this." Here are some examples of some positive coping statements:

- Just worrying about this is not going to help make it better.

- What do I need to *do* to address this problem?

- I can learn from this situation this time, so that I will be prepared next time.

- Take it one step at a time.

- Take a few deep breaths and relax.

- I don't need a cigarette to get through this.

- This will be over with soon.

- Think about being in a pleasant place and time.

- I did it!!!

3. Learn relaxation techniques. You may use any one of the relaxation exercises outlined in chapter 7 of this book. Other options include exercising, meditating, praying, taking slow deep breaths, and eating and sleeping right.

4. Practice all of these skills until they become part of your life. The more you practice, the better able you will be to cope healthfully when you are faced with a stressor. The whole point is to replace smoking a cigarette with these healthier alternatives.

Problem-Solving

Another trick for managing stressors is to use systematic problem-solving techniques. Tackling a problem step-by-step will make your stressor seem more manageable and less overwhelming.

1. Recognize that there *is* a problem. The first step in problem-solving is to acknowledge that a problem exists and decide that you are not going to avoid it.

2. Define the problem in as much detail as possible. Be specific and include how you feel about the situation.

3. Brainstorm some solutions. This means to make a list of possible solutions *without* evaluating whether they are good or bad. The more ideas that you can generate, the more likely it is that you will find one that works. This is a good time to get ideas from other people as well.

4. Evaluate each of the solutions. Go back and rank your options from above in terms of what you think plausible. Think about the positive and negative consequences of each option. There is no perfect solution, but there may be one or two solutions that will work best for you.

5. Try out one of the solutions. You may have to try it out a few times before it works. Evaluate your attempts to see what worked, where the problems were, and what adjustments are needed. If this solution was not effective, go back to steps 3 and 4 and try another one. Remember, there is no perfect solution. Still, at least one of your options should be fine.

Try this procedure for a problem that you are currently experiencing or have experienced.

Step-by-Step Problem-Solver

Example:

What is the problem? *Can't get along with a co-worker*.

Define your problem. Include all aspects of it in detail. Consider when it happens, who is involved, how it affects you and others, etc.

It seems to occur when we are overloaded at work. It makes me upset and I can't concentrate as well. It appears to affect the morale of the other co-workers. The co-worker in question seems angry much of the time.

Brainstorm *possible* solutions. Write down everything that occurs to you, no matter how "silly" or unlikely it seems.

Talk to co-worker; confront co-worker; complain to boss; do nothing and ignore co-worker; ask for a transfer to another department; quit my job.

Evaluate these options by listing advantages and disadvantages to each. Rank the best three to five.

1. *Talk to co-worker.*
   Advantages: Maybe co-worker is upset about something; we can calmly resolve problem; morale will improve; I will feel less upset.
   Disadvantages: What if co-worker gets angrier and refuses to talk to me? Could make problem worse.

2. *Do nothing and ignore co-worker.*
   Advantages: If co-worker doesn't change, I must learn alternative method of coping.
   Disadvantages: This problem has already caused me stress and anxiety, and it will just get worse. The tension is starting to get to the other co-workers.

3. *Complain to boss.*
   Advantages: Maybe boss will just take care of it and I can avoid discussing this with my co-worker.
   Disadvantages: My boss may think I can't get along with others. I have to solve my own problems. Others will think I am a whiner.

4. *Quit my job.*
   Advantages: Get away from it all. Maybe new job will be a more pleasant work atmosphere.
   Disadvantages: Can't run away from problem. Seems too drastic a step to take. I need a job and a new one is hard to find.

As you try each of the best solutions, and identify whether it worked or not, list any problems and any adjustments you need to make. If none works, go back to previous steps and try again.

Tried talking to co-worker.
   Problem: Initially co-worker would not agree to even talk.
   Adjustment: I tried again in a calm manner at another time.

What is the problem? _____

_____

Define your problem. Include all aspects of it in detail. Consider when it happens, who is involved, how it affects you and others, etc. _____

_____

_____

_____

_____

Brainstorm *possible* solutions. Write down everything that occurs to you, no matter how "silly" or unlikely it seems. _____

_____

_____

_____

Evaluate these options by listing advantages and disadvantages to each. Rank the best three to five. _____

_____

_____

_____

_____

As you try each of the best possible solutions, and identify whether it worked or not, list any problems and any adjustments you need to make. If none works, go back to previous steps and try again. _____

_____

_____

_____

_____

_____

Irrational Thinking

Sometimes your thought patterns can contribute to how you handle stress. Using words like "must," "have to," and other absolute language can leave you feeling backed into a corner with no choices. This, in turn, increases your stress. Aaron Beck, a psychologist who studies how thoughts affect feelings, identified several irrational thought patterns that can contribute to unpleasant feelings and stress.

How many of these patterns describe your own worst thoughts?

Catastrophizing. You exaggerate a problem until it feels overwhelming.

Arbitrary inference. You draw conclusions which are not supported by evidence.

Overgeneralization. You generalize from one incident.

Dichotomous thinking. You think in black and white, with no room for gray areas or middle ground.

Negative thinking. You focus on negative aspects while minimizing the positive.

For one full week, try to catch the words behind your irrational thoughts. Often irrational thoughts become unpleasant feelings before you even notice the thought. Don't let this happen. As soon as you feel the first signs of stress that feels unmanageable, stop yourself. Write down the thought that triggered the stress. Then see if you can label the thought as one of the irrational thought patterns. Just seeing it down on paper can help you manage that feeling of irrational panic—*before* you reach for a cigarette.

Catching Irrational Thoughts

Situation and Feeling (*Panic, depression, racing heart, etc.*)	*Thought*	*Irrational Pattern?*
Ex. *I remember another deadline. Heart races, I feel like quitting my job.*	*I'll never catch up. I'm not cut out for this high-pressure job.*	*Catastrophizing* (*It's only one more deadline, but I'm acting as if it's my whole job.*) *Overgeneralizing* (*I'm letting one incident overshadow the many ways I'm doing very well here.*)
_____	_____	_____
_____	_____	_____
_____	_____	_____

Some irrational thoughts touch on deep personal issues. It can be hard to change core beliefs with a few minutes of rational thinking. Still, while you can't change the frustration of human life, you can become aware and optimistic.

Albert Ellis, a psychologist, identified several irrational beliefs that may look familiar. Some of them include:

I can't take it when people or things aren't the way I want them to be. Naturally, life would be great if you could control everything in your life. But the reality is that you cannot. What you *can* control is how you choose to react.

I would much rather avoid responsibilities than face them. It is much easier to avoid doing difficult things. But procrastinating and avoiding only make more work or make things harder.

It is impossible to change the influence of the past. While it is true that you are shaped by past experience, that doesn't mean that you cannot change. Change is possible and desirable especially if some of those patterns don't work very well or cause you more stress.

I hate making mistakes. Striving to be the best you can be is great, unless you can't tolerate making *any* mistakes. This can hold you back from trying something new. Also, mistakes are good learning opportunities.

Everyone should like me. The old saying, "You can't please all of the people all of the time" holds true here.

I should worry about my future. Planning for the future is good foresight, but excessive worrying about things that you may not be able to control will just increase your stress.

Importance of Getting Support

Finally, it is important to remember to get all the help that you can when you feel stressed. Other people can be valuable resources for:

- Information on how they handle a particular situation that may be similar to your problem

- Listening while you vent your frustrations, anger, or sadness

- Encouraging you when you feel as though you are stumbling

- Giving you physical support, actually helping you do the things you need to do

- Offering expert advice in their particular area of expertise

Trying to cope all on your own can lead to increased feelings of isolation and helplessness, and contribute to other symptoms of stress. People who successfully cope with stress always know when and where to ask for help.

10

Depression

The word depression can describe anything from everyday "blues" and sadness to the emotional disorder of a major clinical depression. Everyone experiences unpleasant situations or stressful circumstances at some point in life that can lead to feeling sad and discouraged. Mildly depressed individuals report feeling less happy than they usually do even when engaging in activities that they normally enjoy. They might also report difficulty concentrating on everyday tasks. Moreover, mildly depressed individuals note that their energy level seems much lower than usual. These feelings are usually short-lived and improve when the situation or circumstance changes. Another option is to develop more adaptive ways of coping. It may be during these low times that you have noticed yourself reaching for a cigarette to "treat" your negative feelings or simply to comfort yourself during periods of emotional turmoil.

When was the last time that you were feeling down? _____

_____

What was the situation? _____

_____

What symptoms were you feeling? _____

_____

_____

At which point did you reach for a cigarette, if at all? _____

_____

_____

How did you believe a cigarette would help? _____

_____

_____

In some situations, your symptoms of depression may not go away even after the stressor has passed. You may even notice feeling depressed for "no reason." You may have also noticed that your depressed mood both causes internal discomfort *and* interferes with your personal relationships and your relationships at work. Perhaps you find that you are unable to function as effectively as you used to. If depression begins interfering with your daily life, you may have a more serious type of depression. It has been estimated that during a lifetime approximately 30 percent of adults will experience major clinical depression. In addition, clinical depression is two to three times more prevalent in women than in men, and in people who have a first-degree relative who has a history of major depression.

It is important to identify what *kind* of depression you are experiencing so that you can develop more adaptive strategies to manage it. This is particularly important to you as a smoker since researchers have found a higher incidence of smoking among depressed individuals. Further, those who continue to smoke while depressed are 40 percent less likely to quit during the depression. Therefore, make the effort to improve this negative feeling that you are experiencing, not only as a way of making yourself feel better, but in an attempt to increase your chances of succeeding in your attempt to quit smoking.

What Does Depression Feel Like to You?

The symptoms of depression can be experienced differently by different people at different times. Read through each of the different ways that people experience symptoms and try to identify which "type" is most consistent with your depressive symptoms, either at this moment or during a past low point that you recall.

Type A

Stomach ache

Quite a few headaches

No energy

Multiple body aches and pains

Bodily pain that you normally have seems worse

Poor concentration

Poor memory

Poor appetite

Nausea

Type B

Can't sit still

Feel like you are "jumping out of your skin"

Feel like you are moving at a rapid rate inside but are not interested in doing anything

Worry a lot

Feel irritable

Type C

Want to sleep a lot

Lose interest in interacting with others

Isolate yourself

Don't feel like talking

Tire easily

Won't go any place

Call in sick from work frequently

Type D

Feel insecure

Feel dependent

Want others around all the time

Feel frightened most of the time

Have a knot in your stomach

Cry easily

You may be able to identify with one of these types, or perhaps your depression is similar to a combination of types.

What does your depression feel like? _____

_____

Which symptoms of your depression are most problematic for you? _____

_____

_____

The following questionnaire will help you identify the symptoms and the severity of your depression. This questionnaire is not diagnostic by itself. However, it is a useful screening device to assist you in making changes that can improve your mood.

Self-Evaluation Questionnaire

The following questionnaire was designed to help you recognize symptoms that you may be struggling with. This questionnaire is based on the DSM-III-R (*Diagnostic and Statistical Manual of Mental Disorders*, Third Edition, Revised), the diagnostic manual used by mental health professionals.

1. Have you experienced a depressed mood nearly every day for the past several weeks?

2. Have you noticed in the past several weeks that activities, people, or situations that used to give you pleasure no longer interest you in the same way?

3. Have you experienced significant weight loss or weight gain without intentionally trying to change your weight?

4. Are you having difficulty falling asleep and staying asleep at night?

5. Do you find yourself sleeping a lot more than usual?

6. Have other people noticed that you are more restless and agitated than usual?

7. Have other people noticed and commented that you seem more withdrawn?

8. Do you feel more fatigued than usual, with your energy level quite low?

9. Do you feel worthless almost every day?

10. Do you feel guilty almost every day?

11. Do you find that it is harder than it used to be for you to concentrate and make decisions?

12. Do you frequently think about taking your own life?

13. Do you feel that life is not worth living?

14. Do you feel that there is no hope for things to be better?

15. Do you usually feel worse first thing in the morning and therefore find it hard to get out of bed?

If you answered yes to at least five of the questions including both questions 1 and 2, and you feel that these symptoms are significantly different from what is "normal" for you and they have significantly impaired your ability to function effectively, then you may be experiencing significant depression.

If you answered yes to some of these questions but not enough to suggest a significant depression, then you may be experiencing a mild type of depression. Perhaps this depressed mood is in response to a particular stressor, or because your coping strategies are not particularly effective.

The Cycle of Depression

Often the actual *symptoms* of depression can make the depression itself worse. It becomes a vicious cycle. For example, a depressed person may report having no energy, interest, or desire in doing anything so they isolate themselves or sleep a lot. This in turn leads to feelings of isolation, loneliness, and hopelessness. This can then be followed by negative thinking, or making statements like, "I'm a failure," or "Things will never be better for me." Statements of this nature lead to low self-esteem, which only fuels the fire of depression.

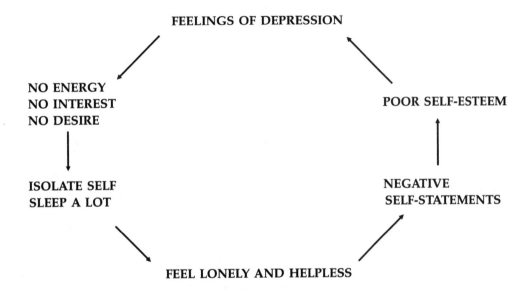

From this example you can see how important it is to manage and/or work on changing each of these symptoms to break the cycle and ultimately improve the depression. Take a closer look at each of the symptoms that contributes to depression.

Triggers to Depression

Just prior to feeling depressed most people can identify *something* that "starts the ball rolling." This can be a situation, circumstance, interaction, or a stressor. These triggers might include:

Divorce

Conflict with significant other

Illness of self or family

Problems at work

Change of any kind (relocation, different job, etc.)

Dissatisfaction with self or relationships

What are your triggers to depression? _____

_____

_____

How You View These Triggers Contributes to Depression

Any of the above triggers can certainly by themselves lead to feelings of depression. However, the way you perceive these triggers can make the symptoms better or worse. People have different windows or filters from which they view things. Your windows are unique because they are formed and molded by your experiences, background, and family environments. Just think how several people can look at one experience and view it completely differently as if they were talking about completely different events. Some people see a glass as half full while others see it as half empty. Some people view tragic events as punishment for things that they have done wrong while others do not personalize misfortune. Some people view setbacks of any kind as an indication that *they* are a failure, as opposed to seeing these setbacks as *isolated* incidences. Such "setbacks" can include gaining some weight when trying to lose weight, making one bad financial investment, or making a negative comment to someone out of anger. The difference between these views is a result of people's "windows," or how they interpret events and in turn what they say to themselves.

How do you typically view situations, circumstances, and events? See if any of these irrational thought patterns fit your own patterns of interpretation.

Blinkering. Do you tend to only look at one aspect of a situation and thereby lose sight of the whole picture?

Narrow view: I hate my job because nobody treats me with respect.

Reality: Tom treats me with disrespect and it makes me feel terrible about being at work.

Alternative view: Although Tom treats me with disrespect, there are others at work who do treat me with respect. I am not going to allow what Tom says to affect my whole day at work.

Overgeneralizing. Do you tend to take one situation and generalize it in some way?

General view: I am incapable of having a healthy relationship.

Reality: The last two relationships that I have had have been with people whose needs were different from mine.

Alternative view: I have been involved in relationships with people who had problems of their own. I am capable of having a healthy relationship—I just need to be sure that our needs, goals, and desires match one another's. I can use the problems that I have experienced in these past relationships as a guide for the future.

Personalizing. Do you tend to interpret events and things that are said as personally reflecting on you in some way?

Personalized view: My co-worker made a comment in front of everyone that somebody ate the last piece of pizza. I am sure that they were thinking that I ate the pizza because I'm overweight.

Reality: The comment was made in front of a group of people and was not directed at me.

Alternative view: My weight is an issue that I am uncomfortable with and therefore I tend to be sensitive about issues of food. Caroline was the one who commented that somebody ate the last piece of pizza and she is not somebody who tends to accuse others. She probably was simply making a comment about the pizza. Unless the comment was directly made to me or I was questioned about it then I need to dismiss it as simply a comment. Just because my weight is an issue for me does not mean that it is an issue for others.

Idealizing. Do you view situations through a belief that things *should* be a certain way?

Rigid view: I should always be pleasant and happy when I'm around my spouse or significant other because people like to be around happy people.

Reality: I don't always feel happy but I put on a happy face to avoid a fight with my spouse. He tends to work longer hours, distract himself when he gets home, and generally avoid me when I show feelings other than happiness.

Alternative view: It may be my perception that my spouse is avoiding me when I am not always happy. I owe it to myself and the relationship to be genuine with my feelings. If my spouse is not able to handle my being genuine than he has to work on being more open to hearing my feelings.

Do you tend to view things in a way not already described? _____

_____

_____

What is the irrational view that you tend to take? _____

_____

_____

How can you rewrite one of your views to describe the *reality* behind it? _____

_____

_____

Now try to write an *alternative view*. Be realistic, accepting, and encouraging. _____

_____

_____

Work on recognizing how you view your triggers to depression. Then you can experiment with alternative views to minimize and control your symptoms of depression.

Negative Self-Talk

In addition to the way you view troubling situations, chances are you have a characteristic way of talking to yourself negatively about them. This negative conversation that you have with yourself probably starts with one thought. This one thought then acts like a snowball rolling down a hill, getting bigger and beginning to roll faster and faster until you have little control over it. For example, you may hear yourself saying,

"I'm not going to be able to complete this assignment for school."

"I should have known that I was not smart enough to go back to school after all these years."

"I am not college material."

"I am stupid."

"I was not meant to have a college degree."

You can see that with each subsequent comment that you make to yourself the self-criticism gets bigger, more negative, and more out of control. In the above example, you start out stating that you can't get *an* assignment completed. In no time you end up with a statement that you were not meant to have a college degree. How does the last comment rationally flow from the first comment? It doesn't. When you start to make negative self-statements you get on a roll that is difficult to stop. The key to preventing this snowballing is to block the first negative statement before it leads to others. This can be accomplished by a technique called *thought-stopping.*

Thought-Stopping Techniques

Various thought-stopping techniques can stop short the snowballing effect of negative self-talk. These techniques include:

- Yelling STOP to yourself (aloud or in your head) when you hear the first negative thought

- Putting a rubber band around your wrist and snapping it when you begin to say negative statements

- Immediately substituting a healthy alternative statement after the *first* negative thought

- Envisioning the snowball and the need to act quickly before it begins to roll away with negative statements

- Clapping your hands loudly when you first hear the negative thought

You will need to use these dramatic techniques at first as a way to stop the natural progression of negative thoughts. With practice you will begin to recognize and stop your self-talk without using these techniques. You will simply be able automatically to change the statement into a healthy alternative, or at least to block the snowball *before* it rolls. The trick is to catch the first grain of "ice"—or negative thinking—that starts the process.

Steps to Beating Depression

Recognize your triggers to depression.

Avoid isolating yourself. Time alone only serves to reinforce the despair that can accompany depression.

Push yourself to engage in small tasks. Depressed individuals often complain of no energy or interest in activities. To prevent this from getting worse and causing you to feel poorly about yourself, set small but reasonable goals for yourself. For example, force yourself to go to the grocery store or to a social function.

Practice the thought-stopping techniques. Don't let your negative thoughts make a bad situation worse than it has to be.

Get support from those you trust.

Avoid all-or-nothing thinking. Usually you will find that the reality of a situation or thought lies somewhere in the middle.

Seek professional help. You don't necessarily have to wait until the depression gets really bad to get professional help. The longer you wait to treat depression the worse it can get, and subsequently the harder it is to beat.

11

Anger and Confrontational Situations

*"Temper is a good thing;
that is why we should never lose it."*

—unknown

Oftentimes people who smoke report that they use their cigarettes to deal with conflict. They light up a cigarette to "buy time to cool down" before losing their temper. Periods of conflict then become "signals" to smoke. It is probably a fair assumption that there will always be situations in your life that cause you to experience anger and conflict. Therefore, it is important that you learn healthy coping strategies to replace smoking as your technique for dealing with these situations.

There are four basic steps in learning to manage conflict more effectively without cigarettes. The trick is to identify your feelings and reactions to a situation, and to learn to problem-solve a solution.

1. Recall Childhood Messages About Anger

How you handle anger and conflict as an adult generally has its roots in messages that you received as a child. It is important to identify the early messages that you may have received from your parents or significant others. For example, was getting angry discouraged? What were acceptable ways of expressing your anger? Was it always important to *win* an argument? Was anger the way that you expressed other feelings such as hurt?

Before reading further, take a few minutes to write down your early messages and experiences with anger and conflict. How do you see this experience still operating in your life today?

_____

_____

_____

_____

_____

_____

After you have written down your own personal messages regarding anger, continue to reflect on how they might interfere or enhance your coping today.

2. Identify Your Own "Warning Signs" of Impending Negative Feelings

Warning signs can be physical symptoms, thoughts, or behaviors that are unique to you. These signs may have little to do with the current conflict but rather be related to your early messages about anger and/or your past experiences that involved anger.

The *physical symptoms* may include:

Increased heart rate

Sweating

Knot in your stomach

Flushed or red face

Throbbing headache

Muscle tension

When you begin to experience these physical symptoms you may find yourself "talking to yourself" about them. This self-talk can easily become a negative evaluation of yourself and how others perceive you. For example, you may feel your face flush and then begin to say to yourself, "Everyone will notice how uncomfortable I am and I will feel stupid." If you have ever said anything similar to this to yourself before, you may recall that it tends to make you even more uncomfortable. Chances are your body reacts by increasing the symptom. That is, your face probably began to flush more and you in turn made more comments to yourself, which in turn made your face flush further. Such automatic negative self-talk only makes the problem worse. It is important to be aware of your own negative thoughts, which you can consciously change to more positive self-statements. Negative thoughts can include comments regarding your physical symptoms or self-defeating statements that fuel the anger. These thoughts may include:

How dare he get on with his life when I'm still suffering.

Nobody loves me.

Why does he interrupt me when I'm trying to work?

I deserve to be treated better than this.

She did that on purpose to make me look bad.

I'm stupid and that is why I never get a raise.

This unfair treatment is because I'm a woman.

In addition to experiencing physical symptoms and engaging in negative self-talk, you may also notice that you engage in certain behaviors when your negative feelings begin to escalate. These behaviors may include:

Pacing back and forth

Fidgeting with your hands

Crying

Blocking out what others are saying

Throwing objects

Raising your voice

Kicking things

Swearing

Name calling

Threatening physical assault

Warning signs of anger serve to prepare you for the conflict at hand. However, if you fail to recognize your body's signs you place yourself in a position of little control and risk impulsive behavior. Remember the last time you reacted in an angry fashion. Were you aware that the anger was building? When you expressed your feelings, were you surprised by the intensity of your reaction? If you answered yes to either question, chances are good that you ignored the warning signals that your body was sending. Learning to recognize these warning signs can serve to diffuse and/or better prepare you for the conflict. Warning signals that are ignored will continue to escalate or "snowball" until your anger reaches a dangerously high point.

The following scale may help you to better identify your own personal warning signs and recognize their intensity.

Low Level									*High Level*
1	2	3	4	5	6	7	8	9	10

Intensity of Anger

Along the scale are gradated warning signals to your anger. As you pay attention to them you can stop the feeling from escalating. For example, you may notice that your face begins to flush when you are told by your boss that you are not getting a raise this year. This might be a warning signal of intensity 3 on the above scale. You then begin talking to yourself and saying, "He is not giving me a raise because I am a woman." When the force of this statement hits, your anger may rise to an intensity level of 6. At this point you may find yourself pacing around your office and throwing objects against the wall. Your anger has now reached a 9. When the first angry feelings hit, try to locate them on the scale. You may want to block them from building. Then again, there are times when the feeling of anger is healthy and justified and you don't want to get rid of it. Either way, your awareness of your anger and its intensity will help you stay in control of it. Conflicts usually erupt when anger quickly rises and the individual impulsively *reacts*. This is probably how you use cigarettes to manage this feeling. You impulsively react to the situation and use the cigarette to buffer or distance yourself from the conflict. However, when you recognize that your negative feelings are escalating you stay in control. When you're in control you are then in a better position to formulate a plan of action. You no longer will need to reach for a cigarette to cope.

3. *Acknowledge the Feelings Regarding the Conflict*

Have you ever been angry about something, wanting only for the other person to acknowledge your feelings? It can be infuriating when the other person jumps in trying to "fix" the problem when you wanted your feelings to be validated *first* before beginning problem-solving. Consider what happened to Sue.

Sue had been experiencing flu-like symptoms for several days. She called her doctor and got an appointment for two o'clock. In order to make the appointment she canceled her one-thirty meeting and left work early. She arrived at the doctor's office ten minutes before her two o'clock appointment, signed in, and had a seat in the waiting room. At three-thirty, Sue was still waiting to see the doctor. She had checked in with the receptionist several times and was simply told that she would see the doctor when she was available. Sue was not feeling physically well and could feel herself getting quite angry. She did not want to express this anger for fear that the doctor might not give her adequate treatment in retaliation for her "complaining." This was a message that Sue had received as a child regarding anger. Whenever she expressed her anger, it was met with disapproval and subsequently she was usually punished by being ignored or emotionally mistreated. With this fear of retaliation, Sue continued to sit and her anger continued to escalate with the passage of time. At four o'clock a new receptionist arrived and she called Sue to the window. Sue took this as an opportunity to express her anger. The receptionist validated Sue's anger by stating, "I can see that you feel angry for having waited so long particularly when you are not feeling well. I would also feel angry if I were waiting this long and not given any particular information about how much longer it was expected to be." Sue could immediately feel some of her anger subsiding simply because her feelings were noticed and validated as real. Once this was done, Sue was better able to hear her options regarding continuing to wait or rescheduling the appointment.

Feelings that are not validated or acknowledged will continue to be expressed in different ways. You may remember situations where somebody resolved the conflict but did not acknowledge your feelings. Didn't that feel unsatisfying in some way? Psychologists frequently hear couples talk about arguments where the conflict was resolved but they walked away still feeling angry. Here is a sequence in which the husband and wife solved the problem but continued to feel angry.

Kim: We have a lot of work to do around the house—and you're going golfing?

John: What kind of things need to be done around here that can't wait?

Kim: The lawn should be mowed, the gutters need to be cleaned, and the laundry isn't finished.

John: All right, if it's that important to you I'll cancel golf for today.

You can see how on the surface this conflict appears resolved. John stayed home and completed the chores. However, later that day Kim left dirty dishes in the sink and John reacted with fury at her lack of neatness in the kitchen. Obviously the anger that both John and Kim were feeling from the earlier conflict was not resolved and therefore it continued to be expressed in other ways. In this next sequence of dialogue notice how these feelings of anger are more directly expressed and acknowledged by both parties.

Kim: We have a lot of work to do around the house and I expected that you would not go golfing today and would help me with the chores.

John: You have never been angry like this before about my going golfing. What's wrong?

Kim: I feel angry and hurt because it seems like you don't want to spend time with *me* anymore.

John: I didn't realize that you felt that way. It seems like you have been yelling at me a lot lately for not doing chores around here and that makes me angry because I feel like I do just as many as you do if not more at times.

Kim: I know that you do chores around here but when you have free time it seems like you never want to spend it with me and that hurts.

John: I do want to spend time with you. However, I didn't think it was important to you because you have been so angry with me.

Kim: Let's work on the chores together on Saturday and then spend the evening together.

John: I'm glad you told me about why you were *really* angry.

Notice how different the dialogue was when Kim directly expressed the real reason that she was angry. It gave John the opportunity to acknowledge his anger and to express how he had been feeling. When feelings and needs are not directly expressed and acknowledged they continue to resurface at different times. Kim continued to feel angry because her *feelings* were not acknowledged, even though the conflict was resolved.

4. Problem-Solving

Once you have begun to understand your own reactions and messages about anger and are able to acknowledge the other person's feelings, the emotional layer can be pulled back to reveal the underlying "real" issue. Without removing and addressing the emotional component to the conflict, it is difficult to identify the issues and to enter into direct problem-solving strategies.

There are four basic steps to problem-solving.

A. **Be concise and specific** when you identify the problem. For example, the statement, "You make me angry when you ignore me" can more specifically be stated, "I feel angry when you roll your eyes and walk away from me." It also helps to begin with "I feel," rather than with "you make me feel."

B. **Break the problem down** into small identifiable parts. When feelings run high in a conflict it is difficult to integrate a lot of information.

C. **Attempt to change antagonism into cooperation**. Try to enlist the other person's help in solving the problem. For example, saying to the other person, "I'm glad that you feel so strongly about this because I need your help in getting this sorted out. What do you think we should do?"

D. **Negotiate a compromise** that will be satisfying to both parties by taking each other's needs into consideration. For example, it may be necessary to divide the day on Saturday to do some of the activities that one party wants to do and some of what the other party wants to do. Notice that in a compromise each party has to be willing to give up some of their needs if they are in conflict with the other person's needs.

12

Boredom

*"Of what use is the eternity to a
man who does not know how to use
half an hour?"*

— Ralph W. Emerson

According to Webster's dictionary, to be bored is to tire of dullness, repetition, and tedious-ness. This repetition and dullness can come from old routines and habits that you have developed. For example, you may have established a routine of coming home from work, grabbing something to eat, watching television, and going to bed. This routine may not have only become boring for you but it also invites cigarettes to remain part of the routine. For example, could you watch television without smoking a cigarette? Could you finish a meal without smoking a cigarette? Do you use cigarettes to manage this boredom of the routine and to occupy empty time on your hands?

Think about the last time that you felt bored or had empty time on your hands with nothing to do but smoke. Were you involved in an old routine? Did you feel lonely and isolated? These feelings of sadness, loneliness, and isolation can be part of what makes you feel bored. If you have established routines that include cigarettes and serve to feed your boredom, and you experience feelings of isolation and loneliness, it is time to change those routines. Changing your routines will help you feel better about yourself and reduce your risk of using a cigarette to fill the empty time.

Steps to Manage Feelings of Boredom

1. **Be aware that you are at risk** for smoking a cigarette when you have empty time on your hands. Awareness of your risk factor will prevent you from falling back into your automatic habit of using cigarettes to treat these feelings.

2. **Change your routines.** A routine that includes cigarettes may need to be changed to reduce the risk of reaching for a cigarette. For example, if you are used to getting up in the morning, starting the coffee pot, brushing your teeth, and then drinking your coffee with a cigarette, you may want to adjust this routine. You may try getting up in the morning, brushing your teeth, drinking some orange juice, and going for a walk before you have a cup of coffee.

3. **Keep yourself busy** with activities that make smoking difficult. These activities could include:

   Washing the dishes

   Doing a crossword puzzle

   Writing a letter

   Sewing

4. **Exercise.** This does not have to be a formalized exercise program. You could take the steps more often than riding the elevator, do stretching exercises while sitting, etc.

5. **Physically remove yourself** from the situation. If you are isolated and feeling alone, you are at risk for trying to find comfort in your cigarette.

   Get up and move

   Call somebody

   Go for a walk

   Distract yourself with an activity

6. **Reinforce your reasons for wanting to quit smoking.** Refer back to your balance scale from the exercise in chapter 3.

7. **Get social support.** Share with friends or family members that periods of boredom and loneliness are a high risk situation for you. Enlist their support during these situations instead of using cigarettes as a "comforting friend."

13

Cigarettes as Reward or Pleasure

"I light up a cigarette when I have finished a hard day at work."

"When I finish my chores I reward myself with a cigarette."

"I unwind with a cigarette after I have finished a deadline at work."

"I enjoy a cigarette when I am reading a good book."

If you have ever said these things to yourself or something similar, you probably use cigarettes as a reward or source of pleasure. At these moments you must also be denying to yourself the harmful effects of cigarettes or you would not be able to "enjoy" the cigarette. Consider this: You are reclined in a chair at the end of a hard day at work. You reach for a good book and your cigarettes. It is your chance to relax and do something for yourself. You light the cigarette. You begin to visualize those 4,680 substances now entering your bloodstream. You visualize your heart rate increasing, your blood pressure going up, and a drop in the amount of oxygen getting to your brain and other organs. You imagine your lungs filling with smoke and droplets of sticky, black tar adhering to your lungs making it difficult for you to breathe. You see the constriction of your arteries and the pressure and force that blood is exerting in trying to get through. You are now at risk for a stroke or heart attack. Do you feel relaxed? Are you enjoying your cigarette? Is this a reward for a hard day's work? Is this pleasure?

Each time you tell yourself that you are going to have a cigarette to reward yourself or you notice that that is what you are doing it is important to counter that thought with the reality of your behavior. Consciously remaining aware of the irony of what you are doing will remove the pleasure from smoking the cigarette and will put you back in control of your smoking habit.

Healthy Alternatives

1. **Repeat the imagery exercise** in detail from chapter 4 regarding the reality of cigarettes and not the fantasy of their use as pleasure and rewards.

2. **Reward yourself by putting money aside** that you would have spent on cigarettes and treat yourself to new clothes, a vacation, etc.

3. **Reward yourself for accomplishing tasks** at work or home by going out to dinner or a movie.

4. **Treat yourself to extra time alone** to read, take a long bath, etc.

5. Reinforce for yourself that you are **treating your body to better health**.

6. Recognize that you are **improving the health of your children** and other loved ones by not smoking.

III

THE ACTUAL QUITTING PROCESS

14

Nicotine Substitution Therapy

Have you ever used a nicotine substitution product (e.g., gum or patch) in your past attempts at quitting? _____

_____

What products have you tried? _____

_____

How did these products work for you? _____

_____

In order for these products to be most effective, they have to be *right* for you and used in the proper way. This chapter is designed to help you understand these products more fully and how they should be used.

Nicotine substituting products include a chewing gum, Nicorette (nicotine polacrilex), and nicotine skin patches, Nicoderm, Habitrol, Nicotrol, and Prostep. These products are designed to gradually reduce the amount of nicotine in your bloodstream to minimize the discomfort of physical withdrawal symptoms. However, before you can make a decision about using these products you must first be able to differentiate between your physical withdrawal symptoms and your psychological desire associated with smoking. Smokers often confuse psychological "urges" for physical "urges." It is important to understand that the physical urges are related to the nicotine withdrawal process. The psychological urge is really more the *desire* to smoke and is associated with multiple social triggers and emotional states (such as nervousness or boredom). This distinction is important because these products are designed *only* to help with the physical withdrawal symptoms and if used inappropriately may serve to actually strengthen the smoking habit. It is also recommended by each of the manufacturers that these products be used in conjunction with other self-help materials or formalized behavioral programs. Although the purpose of this section is to help you distinguish between the physical withdrawal symptoms and the psychological triggers to your smoking habit, it is important to understand that both can exist at the same time and both are important to address in the quitting process.

Physical Addiction

Nicotine is the addicting substance found in tobacco. The 1988 Surgeon General's report states that nicotine is as addicting as alcohol, cocaine, or heroin. This addiction process begins after repeated use of nicotine. Your body then develops a *tolerance* to the drug. That is, your body becomes more efficient at eliminating the drug and/or the receptor cells in your body become less sensitive to the drug. In turn, you need to smoke more to experience the same effects from your cigarettes. When you smoke, nicotine accumulates in your bloodstream. After a period of time without a cigarette the level of nicotine drops and your body "craves" more of the drug. Smoking another cigarette will immediately satisfy the craving, bring your blood levels back up, and reinforce the addiction.

For most smokers nicotine concentration levels show distinct patterns over a 24 to 48 hour period (Figure 1).

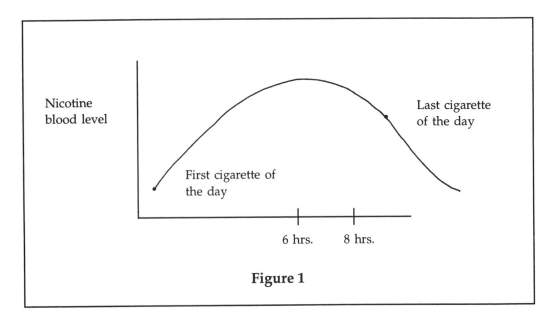

Figure 1

With each cigarette that you smoke, nicotine begins to accumulate in your bloodstream. The amount of nicotine in your blood reaches a plateau approximately 6 to 8 hours after you begin smoking for the day.

When you have finished your last cigarette in the evening and throughout the time that you are sleeping, the amount of nicotine in your blood begins to gradually drop. As a result, in the morning the amount of nicotine in your blood is at its lowest and your body "craves" a cigarette to bring this blood level back up. This is why for most smokers that first cigarette in the morning is the "most important." Then as you continue to smoke throughout the day you keep your blood levels high and your "cravings" low.

This cycle of physical addiction begins when you experience "withdrawal symptoms" and you smoke to reduce these symptoms. This improvement in symptoms is a temporary "fix." Your body then becomes adjusted to the nicotine dose and you develop a tolerance to the drug. With the passage of time your nicotine levels will drop again and your body will require more nicotine to prevent withdrawal symptoms from recurring. The cycle continues.

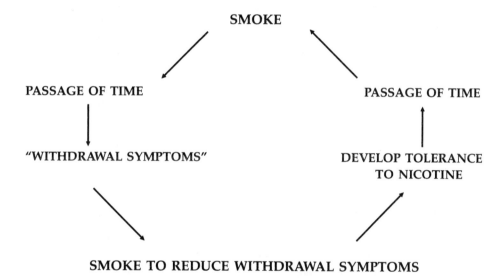

Physical Withdrawal Symptoms

When you decide to stop giving your body nicotine and break the cycle, it may respond through "withdrawal symptoms." These physical symptoms may include:

- Restlessness

- Irritability

- Difficulty concentrating

- Sleep disturbances

- Increased appetite

- Headache

- Constipation

- Dry mouth or sore throat

- Fatigue

- Coughing

- Nicotine "craving"

It is important to understand that these symptoms are short-lived, lasting anywhere from one to two weeks. Almost all of the nicotine will be out of your system in two to three days. The amount and type of symptoms that smokers experience is very individual. Some smokers experience *no* physical symptoms while others report several symptoms. Understanding that these symptoms are temporary and are the body's way of *healing itself* can help turn these negative symptoms into a positive reminder that you are on the path of improving your health. It may be helpful to tell yourself that it is like you are getting the "flu" or a "cold." You know that you may feel bad for a while but with the passage of time each day brings you closer to feeling better. View these symptoms as "important discomforts" in the healing process.

The Symptoms of Healing chart on page 111 will provide you with information about this healing process. As you move through the initial stages of quitting, use the information below as a motivator to remind you that there is a *benefit* to the short-term discomfort, either physical or psychological, that you may be experiencing. This will serve to strengthen your motivation and commitment to the quitting process.

Psychological Desire

You may feel a compulsive desire to continue using the drug nicotine in order to cope with certain emotional states or situations (such as to decrease anxiety or deal with boredom and social discomfort. (Be sure to read chapters 7 through 13 on the smoking habit.) By continuing to use nicotine as a dysfunctional way to cope you reinforce the habit and undermine your own more adaptive means of coping. This cycle of reinforcement begins when you experience a "difficult" situation or emotion and you reach for a cigarette to deal with it. After you smoke the cigarette you may feel temporarily better or more in control. This feeling serves to reinforce your reaching for a cigarette the next time that you experience the same feeling or situation.

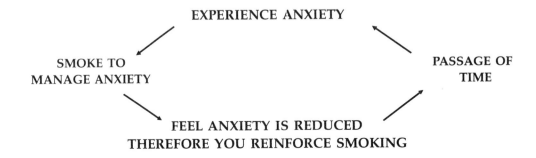

EXPERIENCE ANXIETY

SMOKE TO
MANAGE ANXIETY

PASSAGE OF
TIME

FEEL ANXIETY IS REDUCED
THEREFORE YOU REINFORCE SMOKING

Symptoms of Healing

As this healing process begins, noticeable physical changes occur. The American Cancer Society has reported that twenty minutes after your last cigarette your blood pressure, heart rate, and pulse return to normal. By staying off the cigarettes you decrease your risk factors for serious medical complications.

Carbon monoxide and nicotine levels begin to decrease rapidly. Also, the oxygen supply in your blood increases. As this occurs, you may experience an increase in "cravings." This is temporary and will decrease with time.

Your ability to smell and taste will dramatically improve. You may still be experiencing some coughing as your lungs begin to clear themselves from the poisons. This cough will subside over time.

Your bronchial tubes, which bring air to and from the lungs, begin to regain their elasticity and therefore can more efficiently bring in air. You may notice an improvement in your ability to breathe and subsequently you will become less "winded" or "out of breath" when performing activities. Also, while your body is working hard at removing toxin such as tar from the lungs and repairing nerve endings, you may feel tired or easily fatigued. This will not only improve with time but you will notice that you have more energy than you did when you were smoking.

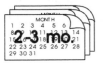

The functioning of your lungs may improve by as much as 30 percent in the next two to three months. You may feel younger because of the increased energy and ability to exercise and do more physical activities.

Your chance for developing infections in the lungs is significantly reduced because the cilia in your lungs have begun to regrow and heal from the damage that smoking has caused. It is the job of these cilia to sweep out poisons and substances that can lead to infection.

Your risk for heart disease has been cut dramatically in **half**. You have also significantly reduced your risk of dying from a stroke, lung disease, heart disease, and other types of cancers including bladder, kidney, pancreas, larynx, and esophagus. These health improvements only continue to increase with the number of years that you remain a non-smoker.

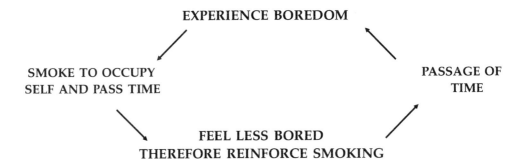

This cycle can be broken when you recognize that you are using cigarettes to deal with emotions and you learn alternatives to cope more efficiently. As you practice using these skills you will become reinforced by experiencing more self-control and belief in yourself *without* the cigarettes.

Cold-Turkey vs. Cutting Down

The question is often asked, "What is the advantage and disadvantage of quitting 'cold-turkey' vs. cutting down, especially as it relates to my decision to use nicotine gum or a nicotine patch?" Consider first the difference between quitting cold-turkey and cutting down in terms of what physically happens to the nicotine in your body.

Cold-Turkey

Frequently you will hear smokers talk about quitting cold-turkey vs. cutting down. What does this mean from a physical perspective? When a smoker quits cold-turkey this means that he or she has gone from smoking his or her normal amount of cigarettes to abruptly stopping completely. The amount of nicotine in the bloodstream quickly drops off. As a result, the body *may* experience some withdrawal symptoms. The benefit to quitting this way is that it is quick and your body immediately begins to heal itself.

The graph that follows describes what happens to the nicotine in your blood when you quit cold-turkey without the aid of a nicotine substitute. The left side of the chart shows plasma cotine levels. This refers to the amount of cotine, which is the end-product of nicotine, in your blood. The bottom line of the graph represents the passage of time. When you quit cold-turkey the amount of cotine in your body drops off quickly, which you can see by the sharp line on the graph.

Cutting-Down or Tapering

Some smokers decide to cut down the number of cigarettes that they are smoking and thereby to reduce the amount of nicotine in the body. The benefit to this process is the

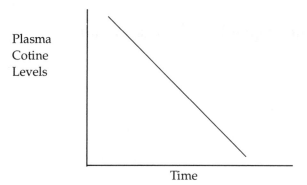

potential reduction in the physical withdrawal symptoms. However, some smokers find that it is difficult for them to maintain themselves at a lower level of nicotine because the body begins to "crave" the original amount that the smoker was consuming. Therefore, they often find themselves going up and down with the number of cigarettes in response to this craving, causing the body to experience "mini" withdrawal symptoms. To prevent this from happening nicotine substitution products were developed. Nicotine substitution products were designed to lower the amount of nicotine in the body gradually to minimize withdrawal symptoms.

The graph below shows how with the aid of a nicotine substitute the cotine in your blood drops off more gradually. The line on the chart demonstrates this gradual decrease over time which *may* reduce the amount of withdrawal symptoms that some individuals experience.

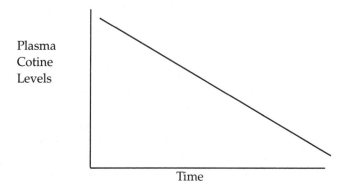

Is Nicotine Replacement Right for You?

Now that you are able to differentiate between physical addiction and psychological urges, and understand the process of quitting cold-turkey vs. tapering with a nicotine substitute, it is time to determine what is right for you.

The following questionnaire is designed to help identify the *degree* of your physical addiction.

Physical Nicotine Dependence Questionnaire

1. Do you wake up during the night to smoke?

2. Do you smoke immediately after awakening?

3. In the morning, do you smoke several cigarettes in a short period of time?

4. If you go more than 72 hours without a cigarette, do you feel physically ill?

5. Following past attempts to quit have you relapsed during the first two weeks after quitting?

6. Do you smoke when you are physically ill?

If you answered yes to the majority of these questions, you probably are physically dependent on nicotine. The higher your number of yes responses, the greater the degree of your physical dependence.

The Nicotine Replacement Decision Chart on page 116 outlines choices for you based on your past quit attempts. Remember that nicotine replacement will only assist you with potential problematic withdrawal symptoms that you may experience. Information from past attempts will be useful in guiding you through your current quit attempt. Begin by answering the question in the top box and following your response to the next appropriate box.

If your answers in the flow chart suggest that nicotine replacement therapy may be a useful addition in your quitting attempt and you answered yes to the majority of questions on the Physical Nicotine Dependence Questionnaire, you may consider discussing with your physician the possibility of using a nicotine product. Remember, these products are by prescription only and as such will need to be dispensed and monitored by your physician.

Nicorette Chewing Gum

Nicorette is a sugar-free chewing gum which contains nicotine. Each piece of the gum contains the equivalent of about 2 mg. of nicotine. By comparison, each cigarette contains approximately 1 mg. of nicotine. However, it is important to understand that the actual amount of nicotine that you are getting depends on *how* you inhale your cigarette and similarly *how* you chew your nicotine gum. In controlled studies looking at how people chew nicotine gum it was found that smokers extracted anywhere from 10 percent to 90 percent of the 2 mg. of nicotine found in the gum. This variability was related to how efficiently the smokers chewed the gum. This is because the nicotine is *attached* to the gum, therefore you must chew it properly in order to *release* it from the gum. Instructions for using the gum include:

1. **Stop smoking.** The purpose of using a nicotine replacement product is to bring the amount of nicotine in your bloodstream down slowly to minimize potential withdrawal symptoms and to eliminate exposure to the other substances found in cigarettes (tar, formaldehyde, etc.). Smoking while you chew the gum would dramatically *increase* your levels of nicotine (and other harmful substances.)

2. Use approximately **10 to 20** pieces per day and do not exceed 30 pieces.

3. When you feel a **physical** urge to smoke, place a piece of gum in your mouth.

4. Chew the gum **slowly** and **intermittently** as this will provide even and slow release of the nicotine into the saliva for absorption into the lining of the mouth. **Chewing the gum too fast may result in hiccups, nausea, or a sore throat**.

5. Chew the gum slowly only until you taste a peppery sensation or tingling. Then **stop** chewing the gum and **park** it between your cheek and gum.

6. When the tingling sensation is **gone** begin slowly chewing the gum again.

7. Keep chewing the gum on and off for approximately **20 to 30 minutes** to continue releasing the nicotine.

8. If you have **dentures** or problems with temporal mandibular joint disease **(TMJ)**, discuss potential problems in using this product with your physician.

9. **Avoid drinking alcohol, fruit juices (particularly orange juice), coffee, or cola drinks** during the first 15 minutes of using the nicotine gum. Using these products may interfere with the absorption of the nicotine by changing the acid content of your mouth.

10. Gradually reduce the number of pieces of gum that you are using. **Do not use the gum as a substitute for times associated with psychological desire or habit** (for instance, when talking on the phone, when depressed, after a meal, etc.). The gum is designed to assist **only** with physical urges and withdrawal.

11. It is time to discontinue use of the product when you can get yourself down to approximately **two to three pieces of gum per day**. Do not use the gum beyond three to six months.

Nicotine Patches

Nicotine patches are a transdermal system that provides nicotine to the body through the skin. There are four major patches available on the market today. Each patch consists of a different schedule for the delivery of nicotine including dosage and duration of use. The graphs on page 117 outline the similarities and differences among the patches.

The usual dosage and schedule for the Nicoderm and Habitrol patches are similar. When using these products, you begin by wearing a 21 mg. patch of nicotine for six weeks. This is then removed and replaced with a 14 mg. patch to be worn for two weeks. Finally, this patch is removed, and you will wear a 7 mg. patch for another two weeks.

The schedule for Nicotrol patches begins with wearing a 21 mg. patch for four to twelve weeks depending on the advice of your psysician. This patch is then removed and replaced with a 14 mg. patch to be worn between two and four weeks. The last patch used is 7 mg. and is worn between two and four weeks.

The Prostep patch is 22 mg. of nicotine and is usually worn for approximately twelve weeks.

Nicotine Replacement Decision Chart

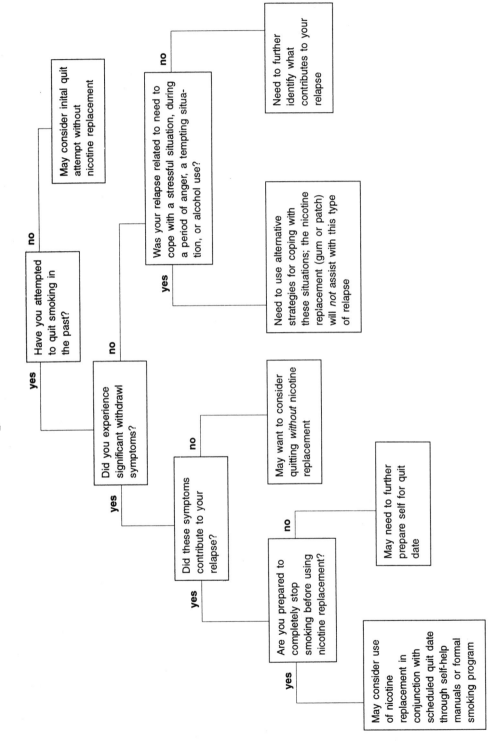

General instructions for using these products include:

1. **Stop smoking.** Similar to the nicotine gum these products are designed to assist with physical withdrawal symptoms by gradually reducing the nicotine content in your bloodstream. By smoking and using these products you defeat the purpose that they were designed for—compensating for withdrawal—and you increase your risk of developing medical complications.

2. Apply the nicotine patch to a clean, non-hairy area on your front or back area above the waist or to the upper, outer area of the arm.

3. Apply a **new patch daily** at the same time to a different area of the body.

4. You can continue to **swim, bathe, or use a hot tub** while wearing the patch.

5. The **nicotine patch should be used with self-help materials or a formalized smoking cessation program** designed to assist with the psychological desire and use of cigarettes for coping. **Use of the patch alone will not address these issues.**

Typical Dosage and Schedule for Nicotine Patches

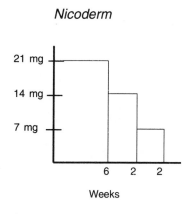

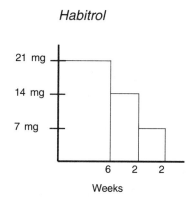

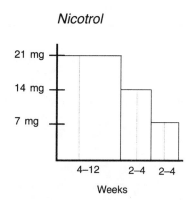

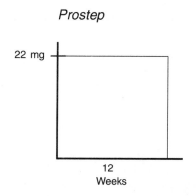

15

Quit Date

Quitting smoking is an act that requires preparation. If you've worked methodically up to this point in the workbook, you may be ready to choose your own personal quit date within the next two weeks. Mark this date on a visible calendar. This will serve as a reminder to you that the act of quitting smoking is not something that you are doing on a whim but rather something that you are preparing for and planning to accomplish.

As you approach the date marked on your calendar, you'll need to prepare yourself for the actual quitting process. Since smoking has been part of your whole existence including your physical self, your emotional self, and part of your general surroundings, each of these areas needs preparation for the quitting process.

Preparation of Surroundings

Cigarette smoking has been part of your life and as such has probably left its mark all around you. In your efforts to quit smoking it is important for you to remove the evidence and reminders of your smoking habit. This will serve to decrease temptation from these reminders as well as to strengthen your commitment to the quitting process through visible reminders.

1. Two weeks prior to quit date, limit your smoking to one room in your home. This room should be the *least* comfortable place. For example, choose the laundry room, the basement, or the porch. Move all of your smoking paraphernalia, such as ashtray and lighter, to that room. Limiting where you smoke will help you to cut down on the quantity of cigarettes that you smoke by making the process more inconvenient. A pack of cigarettes that is next to the couch and in front of the television set will probably be smoked. Further, by limiting where you smoke you also eliminate many of the cues and triggers you identified in earlier chapters. If you tend to smoke when watching television or finishing a meal, you will begin to break that association by learning to smoke without engaging in either activity. Smoking should become merely an act of inhaling and putting out your cigarette and not a part of your daily routines.

2. Clean out your car. Remove all evidence that your car was that of a smoker. Vacuum out the carpet, remove the ashtray and lighter, and discard any remaining cigarettes. After your car is clean, make this a non-smoking area for yourself and other guests who ride in your car. By preparing your car, you will begin to break any associations that you may have between driving your car and smoking a cigarette. For example, if somebody cuts you off when you are driving and normally you would reach for a cigarette, you will now be forced to adopt an alternative strategy to manage this frustration. Also, as a non-smoking area your car will become a safe haven for you when you are tempted to smoke. Now you have eliminated one more trigger or cue for your smoking.

3. Clean and deodorize your home. Since you have now limited your smoking to only one room in your home, you can begin to clean and prepare the remaining rooms for your actual quit date. Get your carpets and draperies cleaned. Remove the odor of cigarettes from your furniture and clothing. Discover and remove those hidden cigarettes that may be lurking in the couch cushion, under the bed, or in the back of the refrigerator. During those initial days after your quit date, you may be tempted by any stray cigarette that you can find. Remove the temptation now before your quit date.

Preparation of Your Physical Self

Once your surroundings are prepared it is time to get yourself physically in shape for the quitting process. As you've seen in the preceding chapters, nicotine is a physically addicting chemical and as such your body may experience some withdrawal symptoms after you quit smoking. To make the process a little more comfortable, it is important to get yourself physically prepared for these changes.

1. Visit your dentist. Get your teeth cleaned. This will serve to remind you that you are about to begin life as a non-smoker. With the tar and nicotine removed from your teeth you are literally starting fresh without cigarettes.

2. Monitor your alcohol consumption prior to and immediately after quitting. The effects of alcohol are intensified when used in conjunction with cigarettes. That is, when alcohol and cigarettes are used together they each bring out the most harmful physical effects of the other. Further, when you drink alcohol your inhibitions are decreased and you are therefore more likely to relapse into smoking. For many smokers alcohol is also paired or associated with smoking. Therefore, when you have a drink you may automatically begin thinking about a cigarette, which puts you more at risk for relapsing into smoking. It may be important for you to avoid alcohol during the first couple of months after quitting until you are beyond the most difficult phase of quitting. Then you can slowly reintroduce alcohol consumption back into your life.

3. Reduce your caffeine consumption prior to quitting. Nicotine acts on the body by changing your metabolism. If you are used to consuming a fair amount of caffeine as a smoker, your body may not be able to tolerate the same amount after you quit smoking. If this is the case, you may experience a jittery/nervous sensation which may not be related to tobacco withdrawal but rather caffeine intoxication. Several weeks before your quit date begin to reduce your caffeine consumption. Remember, caffeine is not just found in coffee but also in chocolate, soda pop, etc. Once you have quit smoking you will then be in a better position to re-establish an appropriate amount of caffeine for you.

4. Get plenty of rest. During your first smoke-free week it is important to get plenty of rest. You probably have been bombarding your body with the drug nicotine for many years. Once you stop the drug your body needs time to readjust without the drug. This healing process can be difficult and exhausting for the first couple of weeks. Plenty of rest will help move you physically through this process with greater ease. Think about this phase as a time for recovery.

5. Drink plenty of fluids. The healing process requires good nutrition and plenty of fluids. Try to drink fruit juices, which tend to cut down on the craving for nicotine for many people.

6. Use healthy oral substitutes. During the initial few weeks after quitting it is important to have healthy foods prepared for snacking. For example, keep celery, carrots, raisins, apples, pickles, sunflower seeds, etc. readily available for snacking. These snacks will help you when a craving strikes and you need something oral to satisfy you. However, make sure that the snacks you are choosing are low in calories and high in bulk. This will help with the craving but minimize the weight gain.

7. Chew sugarless gum and hard candy. During the first few weeks after you quit smoking your throat may feel dry or you may have a "tickle" cough; sucking on ice chips, hard candy, or chewing gum can help. Also, you can use the candy or gum as a substitute when you have a craving.

Preparation of Your Emotional Self

One of the biggest challenges to quitting smoking is preparing yourself emotionally. Many smokers talk about feeling a sense of loss when thinking about quitting smoking. You may find yourself thinking about quitting smoking as losing a friend or at the very least losing your coping strategy. Either way you describe it you may sense the loss of security and control when you quit smoking. To overcome these feelings you need to prepare yourself emotionally for the process of quitting smoking, and for life after cigarettes.

1. Repeat to yourself your reasons for *needing* to quit smoking. Although this has been stated many places throughout this book it bears repeating because it is so important. Your reasons for needing to quit smoking will provide you with the strength and willpower to get through the quitting process. Review these reasons. Reinforce them to yourself several times a day. Write them down and carry them with you. Place them in a visible area for yourself.

2. Plan activities for your first smoke-free week. The worst thing that can happen on your quit date or the weeks that follow is to find yourself in a situation where you are craving a cigarette and you have no alternative strategy available to you other than reaching for a cigarette. Plan activities that are inconsistent with smoking such as doing crossword puzzles, jogging, swimming, washing dishes, going to the grocery store, visiting the library or church, etc. Idle or empty time can be dangerous during the initial quitting process. Stay active and busy.

3. Occupy your hands with other objects. Use pencils, toothpicks, paper clips, rubber bands, etc. to occupy your hands when you feel something is missing without a cigarette.

4. Beware of cigarette advertisements. As a smoker you have probably been bombarded with literature on cigarettes, offered many coupons and rebates on cigarettes, and tempted by magazine and billboard ads. Don't be tempted. It may be helpful for you to analyze and seriously consider what these ads are really saying to you. For example, ask yourself how companies have been able to sell you a product that causes serious medical diseases that can lead to death. Why is it that the individuals who are portrayed in these ads always have smooth skin and white teeth? Nicotine alters the elasticity in the skin and yellows your teeth. Is your health really only worth that 50 cent coupon? Why do cigarette ads always show healthy, young, attractive individuals who are very happy? Most smokers tend to suffer from some effects of their smoking habit such as coughing and more frequent episodes of colds, bronchitis, and pneumonia. Many smokers continue to smoke as a way of dealing with depression and stress. What is so cool and refreshing about tar sticking to your lungs, and 4,000-plus substances being deposited in your lungs (including arsenic, formaldehyde, and carbon monoxide)? After years of smoking many smokers would not be able to participate in the vigorous activities that are shown in cigarette ads, nor are they able to breathe in and smell the fresh mountain air that is shown. Cigarette advertisements are successful in luring individuals into smoking and continuing to smoke by appealing to your perceived vulnerabilities. Everyone wants to be seen as attractive, successful, sexy, and fun. The reality is that by being pulled in by these ads you are risking your life to help the tobacco company make money. If you remind yourself of these realities you will be less likely to be tempted and intrigued by these ads. Rather you should be angry that they are making money at your expense.

5. Never allow yourself to think that one cigarette won't hurt. Many smokers relapse because they fall into the trap of believing that they can control their smoking and one cigarette won't hurt. This is harmful thinking because the majority of smokers may be able to have one for a while but eventually this will lead to two and before you realize it you will be back smoking the same quantity of cigarettes. Further, in order for your body to begin healing itself and to complete the withdrawal process you need to have all nicotine out of your system. By smoking one cigarette you re-introduce nicotine back into your system which delays healing.

6. "Smoking is no longer an option for me." Immediately after quitting you may find yourself looking for excuses to justify smoking. Excuses are easy to find when you are looking for them. However, if you have told yourself that smoking is not an option for you anymore you will need to find another option when your feel stressed or nervous, or when you are finishing a meal or waiting for a friend. On your quit date remind yourself that smoking is no longer an option for you and therefore you must handle whatever situation presents itself to you. This statement will empower you to find and use alternative coping strategies.

Fear of "Losing a Friend"

As your quit date approaches, you may find yourself feeling sad—as if you were about to lose a friend. Frequently, smokers will describe their cigarettes as a good "friend." Smoking may have helped them deal with periods of stress in their life, been a source of comfort when they felt lonely and depressed, and in some ways proved a companion when they felt socially awkward, angry, or isolated. If you share these feelings you may be fearful of what life will be like without this "friend." The following exercise is one developed in workshops. Smokers have reported that when they put this "friend" in a different context they could let go with a little more ease. By following the instructions below you, too, will be able to see your "friend" in a new way.

Close your eyes and picture your cigarette. Imagine that the cigarette is as tall as you are and you are standing side by side. Put your arm around the cigarette. You are now feeling comfort and support from your "friend." You believe that this "friend" will support you, will help you to feel in control, will take away your worry and stress, and will provide companionship for you when you are lonely. Imagine that the two of you are walking arm in arm. You believe in this "friend" and you trust this "friend." You are now approaching a grassy knoll. As you get closer to the hill, you see a hole in the ground with dirt piled around it. Your "friend" brings you closer to the hole. You feel the cold air and see that it is a grave site. Your name is on the gravestone. Arm in arm your "friend" walks you around the hole. You and your "friend" walk around and around the hole. You continue to get closer and closer to the edge of the hole. You begin to lose your footing and you reach for your "friend." You are afraid. You keep reaching and reaching and reaching for your "friend" but your friend keeps walking you closer and closer to the dark hole. Is this your "friend"?

The above exercise can be frightening and sobering. However, it is important for you to focus on the reality of your smoking. A friend would not want you to be in harm's way. A friend wants what is best for you. Although you may not find yourself using the word "friend" when you think about your cigarettes, you may be using and relying on them as such. Remember, a true friend does not just put a bandage on a situation but rather helps to guide you towards long-term coping. Cigarettes may make you feel better for the moment but in the end they lead you closer and closer to years of suffering. Cigarettes are not your friend.

Enlisting Social Support for Your Quit Date

1. Use your support systems. Remind your friends and family that you are going through the quitting process and that it is important to you that they support you. Smokers who have more social support have more success in quitting. Avoid friends or family members who may be jealous of your attempt and success at quitting smoking, particularly if they themselves have failed in the past to quit smoking. Rely on individuals who really want to see you succeed, including those who have successfully quit smoking or who are non-smokers.

2. Be assertive and direct when asking for support. Be assertive when asking that others not smoke around you or place you in high risk situations. Be specific in your request for support or help. For example, you may ask that others be tolerant of irritable behavior during the first couple of weeks, suggest that others not smoke around you, and seek out rewards and praise from others for your efforts. Everyone needs encouragement and praise for persevering through the difficult process of quitting smoking. Don't view this as a sign of weakness.

3. Negotiating with a live-in smoker. Living with a smoker may make your efforts to quit smoking more difficult. Therefore, it is important to work out an agreement prior to your quit date that you can both feel comfortable with. For example, you may request that the smoker not leave cigarettes lying around the house. It may be a good idea to have the smoker smoke in only one room in the house or at least not smoke in your presence during the first couple of weeks after your quit date. Reinforce to the smoker how important quitting smoking is to you and how you value his or her support. Request that the smoker not do things or say things to undermine your efforts to quit smoking. If the smoker really cares about you and your health he or she will want to support your efforts in improving your overall well-being. Sometimes it is difficult for current smokers (even those with good intentions) to really support someone else's efforts to quit smoking. This can occur for several reasons. The smoker may be jealous that you are succeeding at quitting while he or she is not and therefore feel weak by comparison. The smoker may feel abandoned for having lost his or her "smoking partner." This may take some of the social pleasure of smoking away from him or her. Prior to your quit date, it will be helpful for you to discuss these feelings with the smoker in order to prevent any potential sabotage of your efforts and to increase all-around support of you.

4. Working with a smoker. What do you do if a co-worker smokes and is not interested in quitting? It is much easier to negotiate with a family member or friend than it is with a co-worker because loved ones presumably have your best interest at heart. However, this may not be the case with fellow employees. It is important to make a request for support or at the very least for respect of your efforts to quit smoking. Your co-workers may feel that you do not have a right to impose on them or they may share feelings such as jealousy. This is all right. You still have a right to make the request and to work out an equitable arrangement regarding smoking in the workplace. For example, you may ask for a transfer to a work area that is smoke-free. You may find your co-workers commenting on your attitude and saying, "You are so crabby you're driving us crazy—just smoke a cigarette." Remind yourself and them that part of your irritability is related to nicotine withdrawal and therefore it is short-term. This short-term irritability is probably related to physical changes in your body. However, it is important that you not use this as an opportunity to intentionally treat others poorly. Monitor your own behavior and mood. Get distance from a situation if you feel yourself getting irritated. This will help reduce any potential conflict in the workplace. Finally, you may also need to discuss the office smoking policy with your employer. Be aware of your rights.

How Family and Friends Can Provide Support

Friends and family members can play an important role in your efforts to quit smoking. It is important for them to stay supportive of you and your desire to quit and at the same time not to be confrontational or punitive. Many smokers report that the type of support they get from their family and friends ranges from nagging to encouraging them to smoke because their mood and behavior is "out of control." This can leave you feeling like a failure and this discouragement may lead to a return to smoking.

Answering the following questions will help you define specifically what role your family and friends play in your efforts to quit smoking.

What are some things that your family has said to you regarding your efforts to quit in the past? _____

_____

_____

What are they *currently* saying about your present efforts to quit smoking? _____

_____

_____

_____

What have your family members done in the past when you have attempted to quit smoking? For example, have they offered you a cigarette when you got crabby? _____

_____

_____

What have your friends said to you in the past regarding your attempts to quit smoking?

_____

_____

_____

What are your friends *currently* saying to you regarding your attempt to quit smoking?

_____

_____

_____

Is there a difference between the support you receive from your smoking friends versus your non-smoking friends? _____

_____

_____

Ideas for Supportive Family and Friends

- Tell the smoker that you have confidence in his or her ability to remain smoke-free. Repeat this message frequently throughout the quitting process up through the first year.

- Offer to provide support to those quitting smoking by leaving them alone if they need isolation, visiting frequently if they need reassurance, or providing baby-sitting services if the smoker feels unusually stressed during the initial quitting period (e.g., the first couple of weeks).

- Recognize that quitting is a difficult process and as such the smoker may exhibit unusual behavior, such as increased irritability, forgetfulness, nervousness, and what may appear as insensitivity to others' needs. Keep in mind that this will be temporary.

- Keep the smoker *as a person* separate from the act of smoking. Significant others should continue to support the smokers no matter what difficulties he or she may encounter in the quitting process, including possible relapses.

- Offer to accompany the smoker to places that are non-smoking. Discourage other smoking friends from consciously or unconsciously tempting the smoker with cigarettes.

- Be positive. Give day to day encouragement about steps already taken to quit smoking and avoid pointing out slips or problems that the smoker may encounter.

- Be non-judgmental by trying to put yourself in the smoker's shoes. Attempt to understand that smoking has been a very large part of the smoker's life and quitting can be a difficult process.

- Smokers who are committed enough to attempt to give up a physically and psychologically addicting drug like nicotine deserve unconditional support. Plan rewards for your friend during special anniversary times, such as the first week, month, year, etc. These rewards could include taking him or her to dinner, or sending flowers, notes of encouragement, or other gifts.

- What kinds of things could you do to offer support to your smoking family member or friend? _____

_____

_____

_____

Your Quit Date and the Weeks That Follow

1. Visualize and reinterpret your physical symptoms as "symptoms of recovery." In chapter 14 on nicotine substitution you saw a list of physical withdrawal symptoms that you may experience during the initial phase of quitting. Keep in mind that these symptoms are short-term and necessary to the healing process. Try to think about them as "symptoms of recovery." This means that when you are feeling irritable and restless or are having a "craving" remind yourself that although these symptoms may not feel good they remind you that your body is healing. If your body were transparent you would be able to see positive changes occurring. However, since you cannot see the changes you need to use these "physical symptoms" as a reminder or cue that your body is healing. "The pain is healing pain." Each time you feel "uncomfortable" think about what is happening in your body. Use the following imagery exercise to guide you through this healing process.

Close your eyes and imagine your lungs. See the black tar sitting on the tiny little air sacs that makes it hard for you to breathe at times. Each time you feel "uncomfortable" imagine this tar gradually being lifted off your lungs. Each breath that you take feels easier. You feel the clean air healing the wounded lung tissue. You see the 4,000-plus particles that are floating in your bloodstream being washed away. You feel your arteries relaxing and allowing blood to pass more readily through, cutting your risk for strokes and heart attacks. With each passing day you see more and more healing occurring inside your body. With each "discomfort" that you feel you see healing occurring in your body. You remind yourself that these symptoms are short-term.

2. Pay attention to your "high risk" situations. In chapter 7 you filled out a chart that defined your own smoking patterns. Refer to this chart and focus on your "high risk" areas. These are times, such as when you are stressed at work or finishing a meal, when you are most likely to desire a cigarette. During the initial weeks after quitting smoking it is important that you pay close attention to these situations or feelings. Prepare for them and have alternative strategies available. You are most at risk for automatically falling back into your routine of smoking during the first couple of weeks after quitting smoking if you are not vigilant about these "high risk" areas. Try either to avoid these situations or at the very least to have alternative strategies available.

3. Use distraction techniques. When you find yourself tempted to smoke a cigarette get some distance from the thought or situation. Distraction is a wonderful technique for preventing impulsive smoking. Distraction could include physically removing yourself from the situation, shifting your thought to something other than smoking, or engaging in an activity that makes smoking difficult (such as washing dishes, exercising, or visiting a non-smoking friend). It is important to remember that the "desire" to smoke is generally very brief, lasting only seconds. Initially after quitting you may find that the "desire" for a cigarette feels fairly strong and you may "desire" a cigarette quite frequently. However, with time you will notice that the strength and frequency of the desire will decrease. This is why distraction can be very helpful. If you distract yourself for a brief period of time, the "desire" will fade and over time you will not experience the desire as often. Say to yourself, "This desire will only last for a short period of time and if I give into it and smoke I will have to start the healing process all over again. If I can distract myself the desire will pass and I will be one step closer to reducing the frequency of this desire." Reward yourself each time you successfully distract yourself away from the "desire."

4. Reinforce your reasons for needing to quit smoking. During the initial weeks after quitting smoking you will need to continue to reinforce for yourself your reasons for needing to quit smoking. Remember, these reasons need to be specific and personal to you. These reasons will help get you through the periods of temptation.

5. Repeat to yourself the benefits of quitting smoking. You need to remind yourself that good will come of the discomfort, inconvenience, lifestyle changes, and general effort that you are making during this quitting process. Repeat the following list of benefits to yourself several times a day.

Benefits of Quitting Smoking

1. Circulation improves

2. Decreases or cures allergies (smokers have three times more allergies than non-smokers)

3. Eliminates chronic bronchitis (which decreases energy level, resistance to infection, and predisposes one to emphysema) in a few months after cessation

4. Reduces number of cavities and increases chance of keeping your own teeth (smokers have three times more cavities and gum disease than non-smokers)

5. Decreases risk of esophageal cancer by 500 percent

6. Decreases risk of kidney cancer by 50 percent

7. Decreases frequency and intensity of headaches

8. Non-smoking women have less discomfort and less problems with menopause

9. Decreases risk of osteoporosis

10. Increases lung and breathing capacity

11. Increases female fertility by 50 percent

12. Significantly decreases your risk for lung cancer and emphysema

16

Establishing a Smoking Support Network

Support can mean different things to different people. For example, some people find support and comfort alone, others may feel more comfortable with one-on-one support, and still others may enjoy the dynamics of a group experience. What kind of support works best for you?

1. When you feel sad or down in the dumps do you tend to want to be alone?

2. During periods of sadness or depression do you feel better when you are around others?

3. Do you feel comfortable confiding personal information in just one good friend?

4. Does knowing that others are feeling what you are feeling or experiencing the same thing make you feel supported?

5. Do you tend to feel awkward in social situations and generally feel uncomfortable in groups?

6. Do you find that listening to other people's similar concerns makes you feel worse instead of better?

7. Do you cope better with your concerns when you are simply left alone?

Finding Your Style

If your answers to the questions above suggest that you tend to cope better when left alone you may not want to pursue establishing a social support network. However, it is important even if you tend to like the independent strategy that you establish loose support from close friends and family members. This may include simply asking them to give you space or time while you are going through the quitting process so that they understand more clearly what your needs are and are not.

On the other hand, if your answers to the above questions suggest that you are generally more comfortable confiding in one person or you tend to feel awkward in large social groups, then you may want to consider a one-on-one type of support system. A one-on-one system that you may want to consider establishing is a "buddy system" network. This type of network typically involves two people working together to support each other throughout the quitting process.

If your answers suggest that you are quite comfortable in social settings and find comfort in sharing your feelings and experiences with others, and that you tend to feel support in knowing that others are experiencing the same thing, then a group format may be right for you.

Whatever the format, many smokers and recent ex-smokers feel that the support of other smokers who are attempting to quit can be quite useful. You might find that a support group or network can be a helpful addition to your use of this workbook. When looking to establish a support network for yourself or considering joining an already established support group, there are a few things you need know.

How to Establish a "Buddy System"

A buddy system typically involves two smokers or recent ex-smokers who join *forces* to support each other throughout the quitting process. Remember that the quitting process does not just include the initial stage of quitting but should also include an extended period thereafter. This time period may be as short as six months after quitting, up to several years. If you are looking to establish a buddy system for yourself, here are a few things to consider.

You need to locate a "buddy." This can be accomplished by either choosing a friend or an associate that you know is also going through the quitting process. Another idea is to find a smoking buddy through other more formalized programs such as smoking classes. *Wherever* you find your smoking buddy, it is most important that you feel comfortable with this person since this will be the person on whom you will rely for support.

Exchange names and phone numbers with each other and establish guidelines. If your smoking buddy is not somebody that you already know, don't hesitate to take the lead in exchanging names and phone numbers. It is also important to establish guidelines up front as to how you will support each other. These guidelines should be something that you are both comfortable with. For example, you need to find out if phone calls of support at any hour of the day or night are acceptable to both of you. Also, discuss your comfort level of meeting at each other's homes. Would a neutral restaurant be preferred? Next, discuss what you each need from one another. Do you want the other person to help you find alternative coping techniques? Do you want your buddy to call you to encourage you through "high risk" situations? Do you want to provide each other with rewards on special anniversary dates—one week smoke-free, a month, a year, etc.? These are the types of guidelines that need to be discussed initially.

Establish a smoking contract with each other. Sometimes when people put their intentions and promises down in writing it tends to make them feel a greater sense of commitment. Obviously these contracts are not legally binding, but psychologically they do make people feel more bound to their promises to themselves and to the person with whom they are contracting. Below is a sample contract that you may want to use with your smoking buddy. This contract will serve as a strong reminder of your commitment to the quitting process. Therefore, after you have signed it you may want to keep it in a place where you can periodically look at it to strengthen your motivation, particularly during periods of "high risk."

How to Choose a Support Group That Is Right for You

A support group should serve to enhance and strengthen your commitment to the quitting process. To that end it is important that you choose a group that matches where you are in the quitting process. For example, if you have already quit smoking and are

---

Smoking Contract

I ____*your name*____ am committed and motivated to quit smoking because

_____*list your top three reasons for quitting*_____ .

I believe that smoking is no longer an option for me. Therefore, I am making

a promise to ____*name of your smoking buddy*____ that I will not smoke after

my quit date on ____*your quit date*____ . When I am tempted or find myself

in "high risk" situations I will call ____*name of smoking buddy*____ for support

and encouragement.

Your signature _____ *Date* _____

Your smoking buddy's signature _____ *Date* _____

Witness signature (optional) _____ *Date* _____

---

looking for a group to support you as an ex-smoker, the group should focus on information and techniques regarding relapse prevention. A support group can be particularly helpful by providing you with the opportunity to be with other smokers who are experiencing the same thing that you are.

Find out if the group allows significant others to participate in the program. It is important for many smokers that their significant others support them fully in the quitting process. If your significant other can actually participate with you in the quitting process, they are more likely to understand what you are going through and therefore can support you more fully. Also, find out if there will be an additional fee assessed for your significant other.

The philosophy and format of the group should be consistent with your own. In other words, some smokers are not comfortable with groups that use hypnosis or expect participants to interact with each other outside of the group. Moreover, some groups follow a 12-step format similar to Alcoholics Anonymous. While some smokers may really enjoy and feel comfortable with that format, others may not. In addition, some smoking groups are primarily designed to provide information to smokers. The leader may do most of the talking. Other groups are more interactive and allow for active participation by the smoker. These types of groups typically encourage smokers to share their own smoking experiences. The leader may take less of an active role. Therefore, to make the group experience useful for you it is important to inquire about the group format prior to enrolling.

Inquire about the experience and background of the group leader. Be sure that the group leader has experience in working with smokers and with working in a group format. This is important because in order for a group to run efficiently the leader must be able to encourage some members to participate while discouraging one or more members from "talking too much" during the group.

Does the group attempt to personalize the program to meet the needs of the participants? While a smoking group can be a helpful addition to this workbook and to your attempts to quit smoking, it is important that the group can meet your own individual needs. Groups that assume all smokers are at the same stage of quitting and that there is only one strategy to quit smoking and prevent relapse are typically not that helpful.

Find out how often the groups meet and if there is a charge. Some smoking groups that are primarily informational in nature may only meet one time. Other groups that are more supportive in nature may meet on an ongoing basis for several weeks or months. In addition, it is important that you know how the fee for the groups will be assessed. For example, there may be one fee assessed for the ongoing support groups that is to be paid at the beginning of the series with no refund provided for missed groups. There are also support groups offered in many communities that are provided as a free service. Further, for some smoking groups the materials are provided as part of the fee for the group. Other programs may sell the materials separately. These are important questions to ask when you inquire about groups.

How to Find a Support Group

- Contact the American Heart Association

- Check community calendars

- Contact the American Cancer Society

- Contact local hospitals and clinics

- Look for advertisements in the local newspaper

IV

ESTABLISHING A HEALTHY LIFESTYLE

17

Weight Management

When making a big lifestyle change such as quitting cigarettes, you may feel better if you take care of your body and mind in other ways. In this and following chapters, you will learn ways to incorporate good nutrition, exercise, and rewards for yourself as part of your quitting smoking. You may consider making these changes as part of improving your health, in general, even if you find yourself having difficulty with leaving cigarettes completely behind. Think of it as taking control over your whole life and taking the power *back* from cigarettes.

Fear of Gaining Weight

One of the biggest fears of smokers is gaining weight if they stop smoking. For many people, especially some women, concern about weight is a big barrier to quitting smoking. Some of these concerns are real. Many smokers do gain an average of about three to seven pounds after they quit due to changes in metabolism. Others may gain more weight or no weight at all. When ex-smokers gain weight, it is typically because they begin taking in more calories. The changes in metabolism *plus* the kind of foods that smokers snack on after they quit smoking contribute to excess weight gain. Since nicotine is such a powerful drug, its effects on your body are great. These effects include:

- Nicotine tends to decrease appetite

- Smoker's metabolism is altered (accelerated)

- Cigarettes provide smoker with an alternative to eating as a method of dealing with stress, boredom, negative feelings, etc.

- Smoking is an ending to meals: instead of having more food or dessert, smokers are more likely to finish eating and light up a cigarette

- Smokers don't crave sweets as often as non-smokers, according to a study at the University of California at San Diego

When you quit smoking, it is possible that your metabolism will slow down. You may experience an increased craving for sweets, at least initially, and an increase in your appetite. However, the risks of continuing to smoke far outweigh the risk of adding a few extra pounds. You would have to gain a significant amount of weight (over 70 pounds) to have the same health risk as smoking one pack of cigarettes a day. Moreover, non-smokers enjoy such benefits to their appearance as improved skin tone, teeth, and youthfulness.

Good Nutrition

You *can* control your potential for weight gain (remember, not everyone will gain weight) by monitoring your food intake and exercising. It will also be important to pay attention to your thoughts and feelings when you crave a cigarette, so that you can be careful not to substitute high-calorie eating instead of a cigarette as a way of coping. Take a look at the components of healthy nutrition.

You don't have to go on a full-scale diet when you quit smoking. Actually, it is probably not a good idea to make drastic changes while attempting to quit smoking. Make sure you are eating a well-balanced diet with appropriate amounts of carbohydrates, protein, fat, and vitamins and minerals. Keep in mind that your body is in a state of healing and, as such, requires good nutrition. Eating a variety of foods will ensure that you are getting an adequate balance of all the nutrients that you require to stay healthy. Select foods from each of the major food groups forming the lower five blocks of the U. S. Department of Agriculture Food Guide Pyramid (in cooperation with the American Dietetic Association).

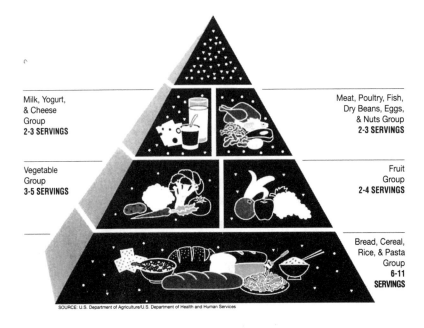

Milk, Yogurt, & Cheese Group
2-3 SERVINGS

Meat, Poultry, Fish, Dry Beans, Eggs, & Nuts Group
2-3 SERVINGS

Vegetable Group
3-5 SERVINGS

Fruit Group
2-4 SERVINGS

Bread, Cereal, Rice, & Pasta Group
6-11 SERVINGS

SOURCE: U.S. Department of Agriculture/U.S. Department of Health and Human Services

Here are some examples of recommended foods from each of the major food groups:

Grain Products: 6–11 Servings

One serving equals 1 slice of bread or 1 ounce of dry cereal or ½ cup cooked rice, cereal, or pasta.

- Rice, couscous, bulgur wheat
- Bread (all types), English muffins, bagels, pita bread, low-fat rolls
- Pasta
- Cold cereals that don't have a lot of sugar added (Corn Flakes, Rice Krispies, Shredded Wheat)
- Hot cereals such as oatmeal or cream of wheat
- Crackers that are low-fat such as saltines, Melba toast
- Pancakes and waffles that are low-fat

Vegetables: 3–5 Servings

One serving equals ½ cup of cooked or raw vegetables or 1 cup of raw, leafy vegetables or 6 ounces of vegetable juice.

- Any fresh vegetable without sauce
- Frozen and canned vegetables
- Vegetable juices like tomato or V-8

Fruits: 2–4 Servings

One serving equals ½ cup chopped raw or cooked fruit or 1 medium apple, pear, banana, or orange or ½ cup canned fruit or six ounces of fruit juice.

- Any fresh fruit
- Unsweetened applesauce
- Dried fruits such as apricots and figs
- Canned fruit like pineapple in its own juice
- Fruit juice (all natural, unsweetened)

Milk Products: 2–3 Servings

One serving equals 1 cup of milk or yogurt or 2 ounces of processed cheese or 12 ounces of natural cheese.

- 1 percent low-fat or skim milk

- Buttermilk (low-fat)

- Low-fat yogurt and cottage cheese

- Cheeses that contain 2 or less grams of fat per ounce

- Frozen dairy desserts that have 2 or less grams of fat per 2 cup serving

Meat Products: 2–3 Servings

One serving equals 2 to 3 ounces of cooked lean meat, poultry, or fish or 1 to 12   cups of cooked dried beans or 2 to 3 eggs or 4 to 5 tablespoons of peanut butter

- Chicken or turkey without skin

- Beef: lean cuts include top round, eye of round

- Veal and pork: avoid cuts of loin and rib, which tend to have more fat

- Cold cuts that contain 1 gram of fat per ounce

- Any fresh fish and shellfish

- Canned fish that is water-packed like tuna or salmon

- Any dried beans, lentils, and peas such as split peas, black beans, kidney beans

- Egg whites and egg substitutes

The top portion of the Food Pyramid is for foods such as butter, oils, sweets, condiments like dressings and mayonnaise, and alcohol. These should be consumed sparingly since they can add a significant amount of calories if you are not careful.

As you can see, the recommended diet is high in complex carbohydrates and lower in fat and protein. Complex carbohydrates are not only healthier for your body, but they also help increase your body's level of serotonin, a neurotransmitter that is involved in regulating mood. If you feel better, you will be less likely to be tempted to smoke as a way of improving your mood. Watching your fat and animal protein intake will help keep your weight and cholesterol down.

Fiber

It is important to add fiber to your everyday diet. The National Cancer Institute is now recommending a diet that is high in fiber (20 to 25 grams per day). Fiber helps soften stool, reduce constipation, and generally improve digestion. This lessens the chance that cancer-causing substances found in foods stay in contact with the intestinal tract, particularly the colon. High-fiber foods also reduce the level of sugar in the blood which reduces feelings of hunger. Some fibers also help lower cholesterol. Eating foods that are made from whole grains as well as lots of fruits and vegetables will help. Below is a list of some foods that are high in fiber.

Good Fiber Foods

	Food	*Serving Size*	*Fiber (grams)*
Breads:	rye, wheat	1 slice	1.9–2.0
Cereals:	bran	1 cup	23.0
	Shredded Wheat	2 biscuits	6.1
	rolled oats	½ cup	4.5
Fruits:	apple (with skin)	1 small	3.0
	grapefruit	½	2.6
	orange	1 small	1.8
	strawberries	½ cup	2.6
	banana	1 medium	1.8
Vegetables:	carrots (raw)	1 medium	3.7
	corn	⅔ cup	4.2
	dried peas, beans	½ cup	6.9
	potatoes	⅔ cup	3.1

Keeping a Food Diary

What are your current eating habits? Use the Food Diary on page 143 to keep track of your eating patterns for the next three days. The areas in which your average daily consumption varies greatly from the ideal are the areas that you may want to target for improvement.

Fluids

It is important to keep your fluid intake at an adequate level. The body requires about three quarts a day for normal functioning. You usually get this from the food and liquids you have during each day. However, when you quit smoking, your body is in a state of healing and therefore will require additional fluids. It is preferable for the fluids to be mostly non-caffeinated. Caffeine is a diuretic which means that it takes water from the body. Caffeine and its relation to smoking will be discussed later. Health experts suggest drinking at least eight 8-ounce glasses of liquids per day. Fruit juices, low-fat or skim milk, and flavored or plain water are good choices. This fluid can also be in the form of soups and broths. The benefits of taking in plenty of fluids include:

- **Fluids help the body get rid of toxic substances.** Drinking adequate fluids helps the kidneys efficiently flush out substances which the body does not need.

- Fluids also help the bowels work better at getting rid of the body's waste material.

- **Fluids keep the skin soft and supple.** This is important for smokers since the skin of smokers tends to be damaged from years of exposure to cigarette smoke. Nicotine tends to change the elasticity of the skin and reduces the function of the sweat glands that keeps the skin moist. As a result smokers tend to look significantly older than their non-smoking counterparts.

- **Drinking lots of fluids will help to control your weight.** Many people find that if they drink liquids before and after a meal, it helps to reduce their appetite.

If you exercise regularly, it becomes extra-important to replace fluids lost when you sweat. Sports drinks are only needed if you exercise extremely hard for long periods of time. If you drink caffeinated beverages, you will have to consume more fluids to ensure that your body gets adequate liquid nourishment.

What You Eat Can Affect Your Mood

Certain types of foods can affect the way you feel emotionally as well as physically. Foods containing caffeine or sugar, for example, can make you feel jittery, tired, irritable, or hyperactive. Some people believe that eating high-sugar foods has been associated with hyperactivity in children. Others have noticed that sugar causes mood swings. Now that you are smoke-free, it will be important to monitor your consumption of these types of foods because your body will metabolize them differently without nicotine.

Sugar

Sugar, as it comes to the table, is chemically related to the basic form of energy that your body uses, glucose. This is probably why it is the handiest food to reach for, and often crave, when you are hungry. When you eat simple carbohydrates, especially sugar, your pancreas produces more insulin, which regulates the amount of glucose that goes into the other organs and muscles. Increased amounts of insulin caused by eating lots of sugar cause the body to have less glucose in the blood. You may have noticed feeling "low" a short while after eating a candy bar as a snack. This decreased energy is due to the low level of blood

Food Diary

For three days, keep track of how many servings you have of each of these food categories. For each category, divide the total serving by 3 to get your daily average for the period. Compare your eating pattern to the ideal listed in the righthand column.

	Day One Servings	Day Two Servings	Day Three Servings	Average Servings Per Day	Ideal Servings Per Day
Vegetables and Fruits (serving = ½ cup, 1 apple, 1 orange, medium potato)					4
Breads and Cereals (serving = 1 slice bread, ¾ cup cereal)					4
Milk, cheeese, yogurt (serving = 1 cup milk, 1 medium slice cheese)					2–4
Meat, poultry, fish, eggs and beans, nuts (serving = 3 oz. lean meat, 2 eggs, 1¼ cup cooked beans, 4 Tbsp. peanut butter, ¾ cup nuts)					2
Alcohol (serving = 1 beer, 1 glass of wine or cocktail)					0–1
Fats and Sweets (serving = 1 candy bar, 2 Tbsp. salad dressing, 1 cup ice cream, 1 order french fries)					0
Caffeine (serving = 1 cup coffee or black tea)					0

sugar in your body. This, in turn, leads you to feel more hungry and to crave more food. When you are trying to manage your weight, eating foods that have high sugar content in them (cookies, ice cream, cakes, pies, desserts, candy bars) will likely increase your craving for more sugar and thus make it difficult to maintain your weight.

Smokers tend to crave more sweets shortly after quitting, while the body is trying to readjust itself metabolically without nicotine. Therefore, it will be important to satisfy the sweet craving without adding excess calories and mood swings. To this end, you may want to try some recipes designed to help satisfy this craving. You may even find low-fat cooking a good distraction from the urge to smoke.

The following recipes were supplied by Leanne Edmonds who consults with individuals who want to continue to eat their favorite recipes but need to cut down on fat, sugar, and/or calories. She suggests a few basic changes that you can make to your own favorite recipes that will help satisfy your sweet tooth without excess calories. These suggestions include:

- Add light or fat-free ingredients (such as light cream cheese, light or diet butter, and semi-sweet chocolate in place of milk chocolate).

- Substitute skim milk in place of whole or 2 percent milk.

- Use unsweetened 100 percent fruit juices in place of sugar when the recipe does not involve meringues.

- Substitute egg-beaters instead of eggs when a recipe calls for more than two eggs.

Lemon Angel Trifle

1 box angel food cake mix

1 box lemon pudding (Instant)

Skim milk

Fresh or frozen strawberries, blueberries, or raspberries

Lite Cool Whip, or other whipped cream substitute

Prepare angel food cake in a 13" x 9" pan. Follow instructions on box for baking time. Cool. Prepare pudding with skim milk.

Cut cake into squares and in a large bowl put in enough squares to cover the bottom of the bowl. Spoon in pudding to cover cake, add berries, then Cool Whip. Repeat for several layers.

Mini-Cheesecakes

⅓ cup graham cracker crumbs

1 Tbsp. sugar

1 Tbsp. diet butter, melted

1 (8 oz.) fat-free or light cream cheese

¼ cup sugar

1 egg

½ tsp. vanilla

1½ tsp. lemon juice

Combine crumbs, 1 Tbsp. sugar, and melted butter. Put a Tbsp. of crumbs in the bottom of small muffin paper cups. Press down firmly. In a separate bowl, combine cream cheese, sugar, lemon juice, and vanilla. Mix at medium speed until the ingredients are creamed. Blend in egg. Spoon mixture over the crumbs about ¾ of the way full.

Bake on 325° for 25 minutes. Top with fruit.

No-Guilt Milkshake

Frozen yogurt

Skim milk

Fresh or frozen fruit

Blend together yogurt and skim milk in a blender. Before the mixture becomes smooth add fruit. Blend for a few seconds allowing chunks of fruit to remain. Top with fruit or low-fat granola.

Apple Crisp

5 cups apples

¼ cup honey

⅓ cup oats (not instant)

⅓ cup flour

¼ cup brown sugar

3 Tbsp. cold diet butter

½ tsp. apple pie spice

¼ tsp. vanilla

Peel and core apples. Slice them into long pieces and place them in a glass baking dish. Mix together by hand oats, flour, brown sugar, spice, butter, and vanilla.

Sprinkle mixture over the apples. Bake at 350° for 25 minutes or until the apples become soft.

Meringue Cookies

2 egg whites

⅛ tsp. salt

⅛ tsp. cream of tartar

¼ tsp. almond extract

¾ cup granulated sugar

½ cup fresh or frozen chopped cherries

1 (6 oz.) pkg. mini semi-sweet morsels

Beat egg whites, salt, cream of tartar, and almond extract until soft peaks form. Place a knife into the mixture to check for peaks. Gradually add sugar, until mixture becomes stiff.

Add cherries and mini-chocolate chips. Spray 13" x 9" pan with cooking spray. Drop mixture by spoonful on the pan. Allow space for spreading.

Bake at 300° for 25 minutes. Let cool and then remove.

Frozen Banana Treats

Bananas

1 (6 oz.) pkg. of semi-sweet chocolate morsels

½ tsp. diet butter

Freeze bananas.

Melt morsels and butter in microwave or double boiler. Put a wooden skewer in banana. Dip only one side of banana in chocolate. Roll in low-fat granola. Re-freeze banana.

Caffeine

Caffeine can also contribute to mood swings, irritability, anxiety, difficulty sleeping, restlessness, headaches, and a pounding chest. It is also a stimulant like nicotine. Because smoking increases metabolism, your ability to tolerate caffeine is increased as long as you smoke. For example, you may have been able to consume three or more cups of coffee per day while you were smoking. But when you quit, the same amount of caffeine may leave you feeling jittery or shaky. You may attribute this feeling to nicotine withdrawal symptoms and be tempted to smoke a cigarette to manage this feeling. But the shakiness might actually be caffeine intoxication. This is actually a disorder seen by many health care providers. Therefore, it will be important to limit your caffeine intake while you are in the quitting process and your body is readjusting itself.

Where's the caffeine?

Here is a list from the *Wellness Encyclopedia* of the amounts of caffeine found in various products such as coffee, tea, colas, and chocolate. The amount may vary according to the brand. Be sure to check the labels of foods and drinks for the caffeine content.

Per 5-ounce serving

Coffee, instant	40–105 mg
Coffee, drip	110–150 mg
Coffee, percolated	60–125 mg
Coffee, decaffeinated	2–5 mg
Tea, steeped for five minutes	40–100 mg
Hot chocolate	2–10 mg
Cola drinks (per 12 ounce can)	45 mg
Milk chocolate (per 1 ounce)	1–15 mg
Bittersweet chocolate	5–35 mg

Remember, if you have been consuming lots of caffeinated beverages throughout the day, withdrawing suddenly may result in some side effects. These include headaches, feeling tired, difficulty concentrating, and craving more caffeine. Gradually taper your consumption and these symptoms will disappear with time. You may want to cut back on your caffeine use before you quit smoking so that you don't have to contend with too many changes at once.

How much caffeine do you consume in a typical day?

Number of cups of coffee _____

Amount of caffeine per serving (check label if possible) _____

Multiply the amount of caffeine x number of cups = Total amount of caffeine from coffee

_____

Number of cups of tea _____

Amount of caffeine per serving _____

Total amount of caffeine from tea _____

Amount of chocolate (cakes, candy bars, hot chocolate) _____

_____

If possible, estimate the amount of caffeine _____

Number of soda beverages (include colas, diet, and any non-cola drinks) _____

_____

Total amount of caffeine from soda _____

If you add up all the totals from each category, you will get the amount of milligrams of caffeine you are consuming per day _____

_____

While there are not fixed guidelines for how much is too much caffeine, remember again, caffeine is a drug and therefore can affect how you feel.

Alcohol

The combination of drinking alcohol and smoking can create a problem for many reasons. From a medical perspective, the combination of alcohol and nicotine can increase the likelihood of developing certain diseases. Each substance brings out the worst in the other substance. For example, cancer of the throat and neck are much more likely if you are drinking and smoking. Also, individuals who consume a lot of alcohol tend to have poorer nutrition because they eat less and the alcohol and nicotine tend to interfere with the body's absorption of some nutrients. This interference of absorption occurs with each of the substances alone; the effect is magnified when the substances are combined. In addition, the incidence for impotence in men is higher among alcoholics and the constriction of blood flow caused by nicotine only makes this problem worse.

From a psychological perspective the combination of alcohol and nicotine is also potentially harmful in the quitting process. The majority of smokers who tend to drink a fair amount of alcohol report that the two go hand-in-hand. It is difficult to have a drink in one hand and not want a cigarette in the other hand. Most bars are not smoke-free and the social environment surrounding bars is a tempting place for a smoker who is trying to quit. Drinking alcohol and smoking a cigarette appear to be closely associated behaviors. Therefore, it may be necessary to hold off on drinking alcohol while you are in the early phases of quitting. The temptation to light up just may be too great. You may want to avoid social environments such as bars that support both drinking and smoking, at least for a couple months. The goal is to limit placing yourself in high risk situations during the initial quitting process when relapse can be high. It is difficult if not impossible to resist temptation and use your alternative strategies when your defenses are down due to the intoxicating effects of alcohol.

Vitamin/Mineral Supplements: Should You Take Them?

Vitamins and minerals are essential to health. If you are under stress, many vitamins, especially the B vitamins, are required by your body. Smokers tend to have lower vitamin levels in their bodies, although the exact reason is unclear. Perhaps they are broken down faster, or perhaps the substances in tobacco smoke interfere with the body's ability to absorb them.

Consider this list of essential vitamins and minerals.

Water Soluble Vitamins

C

B1 (thiamine)

B2 (riboflavin)

B3 (niacin)

B6 (pyridoxine)

B12 (cobolamin)

Folic acid

Fat Soluble

Vitamins A, D, E, K

Minerals

Iron	Phosphorous	Boron
Calcium	Magnesium	Cobalt
Potassium	Fluorine	Chromium
Sodium	Sulfur	Manganese
Zinc	Chlorine	Molybdenum
Iodine	Arsenic	Nickel
Selenium	Copper	Silicon

Special Needs of Smokers

As mentioned before, smokers generally have lower amounts of some vitamins in their bodies. These include:

Vitamin A: This important nutrient helps to maintain the tissues of the body, especially the tissues of the lungs and bronchial passages. It helps to protect against some forms of cancer. Vitamin A is broken down faster in the body of a smoker, so it is important to increase the amount of food sources containing Vitamin A or its precursor, *beta-carotene,* which converts to the active form of Vitamin A while in the body. Beta-carotene is found in vegetables such as carrots, broccoli, and asparagus, and fruits such as apricots and cantaloupe.

Vitamin C (Ascorbic acid): This "miracle vitamin" is required for fighting infections since it is used in maintenance of white blood cells. Smoking decreases the amount of Vitamin C in the body. The best food sources of Vitamin C are citrus fruits, broccoli, cantaloupe, and green peppers.

Vitamin E: This also seems to protect tissue from some toxic substances. Evidence suggests that Vitamin E prevents blood clots—and thus heart attacks and strokes—and keeps tissues throughout your body supple. It should be part of a balanced multivitamin diet. You'll find vitamin E in raw nuts and seeds, cold-pressed vegetable oils, and the germ of whole grains.

Vitamin B12: Mere trace amounts of this vitamin help with stress response in the body; some studies report it is useful in fighting against toxic substances like cyanide found in tobacco. Smokers have lower blood levels of B12 because they excrete more. Foods rich in B12 include red meat, dairy products, and eggs. Be sure to choose low-fat providers of this vitamin, including such vegetarian options as miso, tempeh, and yogurt with active cultures.

Selenium: This is a mineral that is essential in very small quantities. It is used in the body to protect cells from damage by oxidants including those found in cigarette smoke. Selenium also appears to protect against some forms of cancer. Foods rich in selenium include seafood, beef, pork, lamb, chicken, organ meats, broccoli, cabbage, onions, mushrooms, and grains.

Taking vitamin supplements are *not* a magic answer to continued smoking without risk. Your best bet for good health is to quit smoking. It is important to discuss with your physician whether you should take vitamin/mineral supplements and in what quantities. You may have other health problems which may need to be considered before taking supplements because many vitamins can be toxic at high doses. Try to eat a balanced diet as often as you can and, if appropriate, take a daily multivitamin.

Cigarettes as a Food Substitute

It is very common for smokers to say that cigarettes help keep their weight down because instead of eating when they are upset, nervous, or bored, they smoke a cigarette. Is this true for you as well? Keep in mind that the harm to your body from smoking cigarettes far outweighs the harm of gaining some weight. It is true that many people are not so concerned about the health risks of added weight so much as the concern about physical appearance. Since being slim is valued in this society, smokers, especially women, often use this as a reason to continue smoking or "not quit right now." But the real secret to looking healthy, slim, and remaining smoke-free is to recognize if and when you are using cigarettes as a food substitute and to learn alternative strategies. The exercises in which you monitored your personal smoking habits and high risk situations will be useful in monitoring when you may be likely to reach for food.

Food Temptation Record

Refer back to your Daily Smoking Record, which keeps track of when you smoke. (The blank form is on page 50.) If you have quit smoking, list the occasions or situations when you have felt tempted to eat something when normally you would have smoked a cigarette. It might be a good idea to monitor yourself for several days so you can fill in the chart thoroughly.

Time	*Situation*	*What Were You Feeling?*	*What Did You Eat?*

It is likely that you found yourself eating when you weren't really hungry or not at mealtimes. Did you notice particular feelings like boredom or nervousness when you felt "like you needed something to eat"? Substitute alternative activities like taking a walk, doing a relaxation exercise, or calling a friend during these times. Many ex-smokers have found that it is helpful to keep a toothpick or a straw in their mouths when they feel the urge to smoke. Having low-calorie snacks at hand is also extremely helpful when you feel the urge to smoke or have the munchies.

Munchie Alternatives

The following is a list of low-calorie snacks. Have them prepared or readily available so that you can immediately have them when you feel that the temptation to smoke is getting strong. This should help to keep your weight gain to a minimum. Remember, the goal is not to stop smoking *and* stop eating. The goal is to find healthier choices that work for you.

Popcorn (without butter)

Pretzel sticks

Saltine crackers

Rye crackers

Cottage cheese

Apricots (dried)

Carrots

Celery

Prunes

Apples

18

Exercise

Exercise, in any form, is one of the best changes you can add to your lifestyle. As you redefine yourself as a non-smoker, exercise will help your body heal faster. You may have noticed that exerting yourself physically, like climbing a flight of stairs, leaves you winded or short of breath. You may have been able in the past to exercise actively and still continue to smoke. Many smokers have reported that they used to be able to run, swim, or play sports and still smoke without feeling out of shape. But after years of smoking, this was no longer true. Continued smoking affects your lungs' ability to work efficiently. The tar from the tobacco accumulates in your bronchial sacs, thereby restricting air exchange. Adding exercise to your quit-smoking program will benefit you in several ways:

- Exercise will help your body, especially the lungs, clear out the toxic substances from cigarettes

- Exercise will help you fight potential weight gain after you quit smoking

- Exercise can serve as an overall relaxation method—the more you exercise, the less tension you will feel, thereby reducing your desire to smoke

- Exercise is an effective distraction or alternative to smoking—it is difficult to smoke if you are doing something very active

Regular exercise is also associated with myriad other benefits, both physical and psychological. Exercise

- Improves flexibility, endurance, and muscle strength

- Reduces muscle aches and tension

- Reduces potential for back problems

- Helps fight coronary artery disease

- Reduces fatigue, increases energy level

- Improves bowel functioning

- Increases production of endorphins, your body's natural substance that improves your mood, promotes a feeling of well-being, and combats pain

- Improves sleep

- Helps in managing stress more effectively

- Improves premenstrual symptoms and menstrual cramps

- Decreases feelings of anxiety, depression

- Improves body image

- Improves self-esteem

Why It's Hard to Start

As you can see, there are lots of great reasons to incorporate an exercise program into your lifestyle. However, you are not alone if you have not done so thus far, or if you have been making excuses to delay beginning to exercise. If you are not currently exercising, what are the reasons? If you really think about it, you may be able to answer for yourself why these are probably just excuses. Below are some common reasons why many people say they don't exercise. Circle the ones that apply to you. In the column next to each excuse, come up with a counterargument or a solution to the problem.

Obstacles to Exercising	*Counterarguments and Solutions*
I don't have the time.	***Example:*** *I make time for other priorities in my life. I will make exercise a high priority and make time for it each day.* **Your solution:** _____ _____
I'm too tired.	***Example:*** *I will feel tired at first but exercising regularly will improve my energy level and endurance.* **Your solution:** _____ _____

I'll start tomorrow.

Example: *If I keep putting it off until tomorrow, I'll never start. Why not start now, get it over with, and feel like I accomplished something?*

Your solution:_____

_____

I'm already too out of shape.

Example: *I'm out of shape because I don't exercise. It is never too late to get into shape.*

Your solution:_____

_____

It will be hard and painful.

Example: *It will be difficult at first, but I will soon be in better shape and exercise will feel good. I will start slowly at first.*

Your solution:_____

_____

I don't feel good.

Example: *Unless I am really sick, like having a fever or other serious illness, exercise will help me feel better. I can exercise at a slow pace. If I am seriously ill, I will call my doctor.*

Your solution:_____

_____

I don't like to exercise alone.

Example: *I can join a health club where I can meet new people or I can ask my spouse or a friend to join me.*

Your solution:_____

_____

I don't have the proper equipment.

Example: *I don't need to have fancy equipment or clothes to exercise. Simply walking is a good exercise and I can wear loose, comfortable clothing and walking shoes.*

Your solution:_____

_____

Beginning an Exercise Program

It is important to go slowly at the start of an exercise regimen. As you go through the process of quitting smoking, initially your body will be undergoing adjustment to functioning without nicotine. Therefore, suddenly adding vigorous exercise may be too overwhelming. The following precautions are recommended:

- If you have a heart condition, high blood pressure, history of dizziness, arthritis, or other medical problem, it is important to consult with your physician first.

- If you are over 40 years old and not used to exercise, begin especially gradually.

- Use appropriate shoes and clothing to reduce chance of injury.

- Try not to exercise in very hot, humid conditions to prevent heat stroke; wear loose, very light clothing in hot weather.

- Wear a hat, gloves, and several layers of light clothing if exercising in cold weather.

- Be sure to warm up and cool down by stretching and jogging in place.

- Do not exercise vigorously for at least two hours after eating and do not eat for at least 20 minutes after exercising.

- Stop exercising if you feel sick or have any unfamiliar physical symptoms.

Don't think that running and jogging or weight lifting are the best and only forms of exercise. These activities may not be suitable for you anyway. There are many activities you can do that will exercise your body and keep you interested. Choose some activities from the list below that you already do or that you might like to do:

_____	fast walking	_____	dancing
_____	swimming	_____	tennis
_____	racquetball	_____	rollerblading
_____	baseball	_____	basketball
_____	ice skating	_____	bowling
_____	skiing	_____	cross-country skiing
_____	bicycling	_____	stationary cycling
_____	calisthenics	_____	aerobics
_____	volleyball	_____	golf
_____	weight training	_____	jumping rope

Many of the activities that you may do around the house also give your body exercise. How many of the following activities do you do regularly?

_____ vacuuming	_____ shoveling snow
_____ mopping floors	_____ scrubbing bathrooms
_____ mowing lawn	_____ raking leaves
_____ painting house	_____ gardening
_____ washing car	_____ grocery shopping

Aerobic Exercise

Aerobic exercise will increase your endurance and cardiovascular efficiency. This is especially important for ex-smokers trying to get back into shape. Try to get aerobic exercise at least *three times per week* for maximum benefit. You should aim to exercise for at least 30

Target Heart Rate During Exercise

Age	Target Zone (beats per minute)	Maximum Heart Rate
20	120–160	200
25	117–156	195
30	114–152	190
35	111–148	185
40	108–144	180
45	105–140	175
50	102–136	170
55	99–132	165
60	96–128	160
65	93–124	155
70	90–120	150
75	87–116	145
80	84–112	140
85	81–108	135

minutes, keeping your heart rate in the target range outlined in the table on page 157 for about 20 minutes. If you are not used to this type of exercise and are just getting started, exercise for as many minutes as you can. When you feel that you can exercise for 5 to 10 minutes, then slowly add more time progressively each week until you can sustain at least 30 minutes of aerobic exercise. *Remember to monitor your body for any symptoms of stress.*

To find out what your heart rate is, check your pulse for 10 seconds and multiply by six. To check your pulse, you can place the tips of the first two fingers on the left or right carotid arteries (blood vessels in your neck) or on the inside wrist right below the base of your thumb. To check your heart rate during exercise, take your pulse immediately after exercising. Don't worry if your heart rate is not in the target zone yet. It will get there with time and consistency. If you are not consistent with your exercise, it will take longer to get into shape and you will be likely to feel that exercise is more tiring and tedious.

If you are not going to or cannot run, jog, or swim, brisk walking is the best form of aerobic exercise. You can do this at any time. If the weather where you live is not conducive to walking outside, you can walk on an indoor track or at your local shopping mall. The goal of exercise is to help you remain fit. Do yourself a life-saving favor, and make special efforts to do at least some physical activity every day. This will definitely aid in your efforts to quit smoking and to maintain a smoke-free lifestyle.

V

Maintaining a Smoke-Free Lifestyle

19

Relapse Prevention

"The great question is not whether you have failed but whether you are content with failure."

—Author unknown

Now that you have actually quit smoking, maintaining a smoke-free lifestyle becomes extremely important. *Relapse* refers to a setback in your efforts to remain smoke-free. Don't be upset if you have a slip and smoke after your quit date. Think of this slip as just a *temporary* setback. You have not failed in your effort to quit. Many successful ex-smokers made several attempts at quitting before finally succeeding. So don't use a lapse back into smoking as an excuse to give up. Rather, to examine the situation that led you to feel that you needed to smoke and learn from this. You may need to substitute another strategy more strongly than you originally believed was necessary. This chapter will help you manage the potential for slips.

Immediate Coping

Saul Shiffman proposes that a few general coping strategies can sustain you whenever you are tempted to smoke. They are avoiding, escaping, distracting, and delaying. Try these especially during the first few weeks.

1. **Avoid** the situations that are particularly high risk for you. You should have identified them when you filled out the Daily Smoking Record in chapter 6 while preparing to quit. Try to avoid as many of these situations as possible,

especially during the first few weeks after quitting. For example, if you know that every time you drink coffee, you *have* to smoke, then avoid drinking coffee for a while. Many smokers report that social situations where alcohol is served are difficult (alcohol loosens your inhibitions making you more likely to give in). It is true, however, that avoidance will be difficult at times since many situations are unavoidable.

2. Since you cannot avoid all situations (and wouldn't want to), you could try to **escape** from the situation that is strongly tempting you. This could mean taking a short walk or leaving a bar or party early if there are a lot of smokers there.

3. **Distract** yourself. You can accomplish this by doing something else with your hands or breathing deeply. Or you can distract your mind by actively thinking about something else like what you will be doing over the weekend or what you are going to cook for dinner.

4. Wait out the craving. If you **delay** the craving, it should only last a few minutes before it passes. Tell yourself that you are going to wait for a while, do something else, and the craving will be gone. Keep repeating this each time you get a craving throughout the day. It might help to visualize the craving as a wave that you can ride out, and then watch subside again.

Specific Strategies

If You Set a Quit Date But Have Not Followed Through

This may be because you don't feel that you are ready to give up cigarettes just yet. You may be doubting your ability to handle stress in your life without cigarettes. Or you may be concerned about withdrawal symptoms.

What are your reasons for not being able to follow through with your quit date? _____

_____

_____

_____

_____

What to do:

- Re-examine your motivation. Look at the reasons for quitting which you listed at the beginning of the workbook. These reasons should outweigh the reasons to smoke.

- Review the list of common excuses again. Are you using one of these?

- Go back and review steps to improve your belief in your ability to quit smoking. This is also in chapter 3 on motivation.

- If you are concerned about withdrawal symptoms, especially if you are a heavy smoker, read the information provided in chapter 14 on nicotine substitution therapy.

- Consider at least cutting back on your smoking. You can use the Daily Smoking Record in chapter 6 to determine your cigarette patterns and cut back by not smoking the cigarettes which you rated as 3 or 4.

If You Have Made it a Couple of Weeks Past Your Quit Date But Feel Strongly Tempted to Smoke Often

Congratulations! You have succeeded in getting past the physical withdrawal symptoms. If you have frequent, strong temptations to smoke, this is natural. This is because of the psychological addiction where cigarettes become associated with so many aspects of your life. But this will decrease with time. That doesn't mean that you will never feel the urge to smoke, but with time and practice of alternative strategies, you will be more able to resist that urge. And as cigarettes become replaced by other strategies, they will no longer be an essential part of your life.

What to do:

- The following Daily Coping Record is similar to the Daily Smoking Record you used to keep track of your smoking patterns. You should have been able to identify some times or patterns when you smoked more or were not able to do without a cigarette (those times when you rated the cigarette as 1 or 2). These times and situations are your high risk situations. Now that you have quit, it is likely that these very same situations will cause you to have a strong urge to smoke. Use this new chart to make a note of these times.

- The Daily Coping Record has two additional columns after the column where you rated how important each cigarette was to you. In the column titled "substitute coping strategy," write down what you did to cope instead of smoking a cigarette.

- In the next column, check whether it worked or not. You may choose one or more coping strategies from the lists on pages 165–166 or use your own. The first list contains suggestions of things you can *do* when tempted to smoke. The second list contains things you can say to yourself. You may find it helpful to use ideas from both lists simultaneously.

Daily Coping Record

Cig. #	SITUATION/PLACE					ACTIVITY					FEELING							HOW IMPORTANT IS THIS CIGARETTE?	SUBSTITUTE COPING STRATEGY	LIST OF WHICH STRATEGIES WORKED FOR YOU AND WHICH DID NOT	
	WORK	HOME	CAR	BAR	OTHER (WHERE?)	EATING	WATCHING TV	DRINKING COFFEE	DRINKING ALCOHOL	OTHER (WHAT?)	ANGRY	BORED	DEPRESSED	SAD	NERVOUS	RELAXED	OTHER (HOW?)	VERY IMPORTANT 1 2 3 4 CAN DO WITHOUT THIS CIGARETTE — SMOKE THE CIGARETTE / DO NOT SMOKE THE CIGARETTE		WORKED	DID NOT

Quick Fix Coping Strategies

Things You Can Do

1. Do relaxation exercises.
2. Leave the situation for a short while.
3. Chew gum.
4. Munch on low-calorie snacks like plain popcorn.
5. Go to a place where smoking is not allowed.
6. Take a walk.
7. Exercise.
8. Listen to your favorite music.
9. Drink fruit juice, water, or club soda with lemon.
10. Take a hot bath.
11. Don't drink alcohol or coffee for a short period.
12. Call a friend for support.
13. Brush your teeth.
14. Take up a new hobby that involves using your hands, like knitting.
15. Do some gardening.

Your own strategies: _____.

_____

_____

Things to Think About or Say to Yourself

1. Think about how many ways quitting will improve your health.
2. Think about how not smoking will help your loved ones.
3. Go over your reasons for quitting.
4. Imagine yourself as a non-smoker.
5. Think about how much better food tastes when you are not smoking.
6. "I can manage this without a cigarette."
7. "I don't want to go through withdrawal symptoms again."
8. "I have made it this far."

9. "I'm only going to focus on what I'm doing, not that I need a cigarette."

10. "I just have to take it one day at a time."

11. "I just have to take it one cigarette at a time."

12. "Smoking is *not* an option for me."

13. "My lungs are getting healthier."

14. "I can breathe better."

15. "NO!!!"

Your own: _____

_____

_____

Keep At It

These coping strategies and any others you use must be practiced repeatedly in order for you to get good at using them when you feel tempted to smoke. Remember, smoking had become an automatic habit and therefore you probably were smoking many of your cigarettes without consciously thinking about it. In order for you to be successful in your efforts to remain smoke-free, it is important that you make a conscious decision *not* to smoke each and every time you feel an urge to smoke.

If you note from examining your charts that you are having difficulty fighting off those urges because you are stressed, nervous, or experiencing some other emotional upset, refer back to chapters 7 through 13 to help manage these feelings. Cigarettes are not a good solution, so you may have to address some more serious issues in your life to get away from them.

20

Nurturing Yourself

Now that you have quit smoking, it is important to take care of yourself during this time. You have succeeded in tackling one of the most difficult habits to break and you deserve to be congratulated. There are several things you can do to nurture yourself during the quitting process and afterwards. It will go a long way towards maintaining a healthy lifestyle.

- Be sure to get plenty of rest.

- Try to get some form of exercise as often as you can.

- Eat a well-balanced diet as often as you can and supplement with vitamins.

- Start enjoying some of your favorite activities.

- Treat yourself to some extra time alone with no pressures.

- Do relaxation exercises, deep breathing, and meditation to relax you.

- Give yourself positive messages.

- Tell family and friends to congratulate you.

Rewarding Yourself

Sometimes it helps to *actually* reward yourself as you go through the quitting process. Some suggestions include:

- For each day or week that you are smoke-free, set aside the money that you would have spent on cigarettes. At the end of the month, use that money to buy something for yourself, like new clothes or new music.

- Or save the money until you have enough to take a vacation or make a large purchase.

- At the end of each week of remaining smoke-free, go out to dinner or a movie with family or friends. The support people that you identified in the social support chapter can help you with this.

- Fantasize about what you could do with the money that you used to spend on cigarettes.

  number of packs per day x cost per pack = _____

  cost per day x 30 = cost per month = _____

  cost per day x 365 = cost per year = _____

  What could you buy or how else could you spend this money? _____

  _____

A Final Note

If you have succeeded in working through all of this workbook and remain smoke-free, congratulations. Feel free to refer back as needed to individual chapters and sections for any information that will help you maintain a healthy, smoke-free lifestyle.

If you have not been as successful as you had hoped, this book will be a good resource to try again when you are ready. Keep trying: The secret to breaking a habit and old patterns is persistence.

References

American Cancer Society. *Cancer Facts and Figures—1991.* American Cancer Society, 1991.

American Heart Association. *Heart and Stroke Facts.* American Heart Association, 1991.

"Are You Eating Right?" *Consumer Reports* (1992): 644–655.

Bandura, A. "Self-efficacy: Toward a Unifying Theory of Behavior Change." *Psychological Review* 84 (1977): 191–215.

Beck, A. T., Rush, A. J., Shaw, B. F., and Emery, G. *Cognitive Therapy of Depression.* New York: Guilford, 1979.

Bernstein, D. A. and Barkovec, J. D. *Progressive Muscle Relaxation Training: A Manual for the Helping Profession.* Champaign, Ill: Research Press, 1973.

Blitzer, P., et. al. "The Effect of Smoking Cessation on Body Weight." *Journal of Chronic Diseases* 30 (1977): 415–429.

Bonham, G. S. and Wilson, R. A. "Children's Health in Families with Cigarette Smokers." *American Journal of Public Health* 71 (1981): 290–293.

Bourne, E. J. *The Anxiety & Phobia Workbook.* Oakland, CA: New Harbinger Publications, 1990.

Boyd, E. J. "Smoking Impairs Therapeutic Gastric Inhibition." *Lancet* (Jan. 1983): 95–97.

Byrd, J. C., Shapiro, R. S., and Schiedermayer, D. L. "Passive Smoking: A Review of Medical and Legal Issues." *American Journal of Public Health* 79, no. 2 (1989): 209–215.

Chesebro, M. J. "Passive Smoking." *American Family Physician* 37, no. 5 (1988): 212–218.

Coates, T. J. and Li, V. C. "Does Smoking Cessation Lead to Weight Gain?" *American Journal of Public Health* 73 (1983): 1303–1304.

Copeland, M. E. with McKay, M. *The Depression Workbook.* Oakland, CA: New Harbinger Publications, 1992.

Davis M., Eshelman, E. R., and McKay, M. *The Relaxation & Stress Reduction Workbook*. 3rd edition. Oakland, CA: New Harbinger Publications, 1988.

Deanfield, J., Wright, C., Krikler, S., et. al. "Cigarette Smoking and the Treatment of Angina with Propanolol, Aternolol, and Nifedipine." *New England Journal of Medicine* 310 (1984): 951–954.

Ellis, A. and Harper, R. A. *A New Guide to Rational Living*. Hollywood, CA: Wilshire Book Co., 1975.

Fanning, P. *Visualization for Change*. Oakland, CA: New Harbinger Publications, 1988.

Ferguson, T. *The Smoker's Book of Health*. New York: G.P. Putnam's Sons, 1987.

Fiore, M., Novotny, T. E., Pierce, J. P., Hatziandreau, E. J., Petel, K. M., and Davis, R. M. "Trends in Cigarette Smoking in the United States—the Changing Influence of Gender and Race." *Journal of the American Medical Association* 261 (1989): 49–55.

Grunberg, N. E. "The Effects of Nicotine and Cigarette Smoking Consumption and Taste Preferences." *Journal of Addictive Behaviors* 7, no. 4 (1982): 317–331.

Harvey, J. R. "Diaphragmatic Breathing: A Practical Technique for Breath Control." *The Behavior Therapist* 1 (1979): 13–14.

Holmes, T. H. and Rahe, R. H. "The Social Readjustment Rating Scale." *Journal of Psychosomatic Research* 11 (1967): 216.

Janerich, D. T., Thompson, W. D., Varela, L.R., et. al. "Lung Cancer and Exposure to Tobacco Smoke in the Household." *New England Journal of Medicine* 323 (1990): 632–636.

Jones, R. M., "Smoking Before Surgery: The Case for Stoping." *British Medical Journal* 290 (1985): 1763–1764.

Knott, V. J. and Venables, P. H. "EEG Correlates of Non-Smokers, Smokers, Smoking and Smoking Deprivation." *Psychophysiology* 14 (1977): 150–156.

Kusinitz, I., Fine, M., and Editors of Consumer Reports Books. *Physical Fitness for Practically Everybody: The Consumers Union Report on Exercise*. Mount Vernon, NY: Consumers Union, 1983.

Lichtenstein, E. "The Smoking Problem: A Behavioral Perspective." *Journal of Consulting and Clinical Psychology* 50 (1982): 804–819.

Lipman, A. "How Smoking Interferes with Drug Therapy." *Modern Medicine* (Aug. 1985): 141–142.

Marlatt, G. A. and Gordon, J. R. *Relapse Prevention: Maintainance Strategies in the Treatment of Addictive Behaviors*. New York: Guilford Press, 1985.

McKay, M., Davis, M., and Fanning, P. *Thoughts & Feelings: The Art of Cognitive Stress Intervention*. Oakland, CA: New Harbinger Publications, 1981.

McKay, M., Rogers, P. D., and McKay, J. *When Anger Hurts: Quieting the Storm Within*. Oakland, CA: New Harbinger Publications, 1989.

Meichenbaum, D. and Turk, D. C. *Facilitating Treatment Adherence: A Practitioner's Guidebook.* New York: Plenum Press, 1987.

Milton, E. E. and Hammond, C. H. "The Effects of Smoking on Packed Cell Volume, Red Blood Cell Counts, Hemoglobin, and Platelet Count." *Canadian Medical Association Journal* 75 (1956): 520–523.

Netzer, C. T. *The Complete Book of Food Counts.* 2nd ed. New York: Dell Publishing, 1991.

Orleans, C. T. and Slade. J. (eds). *Nicotine Addiction: Principles and Management.* New York: Oxford Press, 1993.

Rippe, J. M. and Amend, P. *The Exercise Exchange Program.* New York: Simon and Schuster, 1992.

Selye, H. *The Stress of Life.* New York: McGraw-Hill, 1956.

Shiffman, S., et. al. "Preventing Relapse in Ex-Smokers: A Self-Management Approach." In Marlatt and Gordon (eds). *Relapse Prevention: Maintainance Strategies in the Treatment of Addictive Behaviors.* New York: Guilford Press, 1985.

Stockwell, T. R., Rutley, R., and Clark, K. "Pesticides and Other Chemicals in Cigarette Tobacco" (letter). *Medical Journal of Australia* 157, no. 1 (Jul. 6, 1992): 68.

U.S. Department of Agriculture and U.S. Department of Health and Human Services. "Nutrition and Your Health: Dietary Guidelines for Americans." 3rd ed. *Home and Garden Bulletin No. 232.* Washington D.C.: Government Printing Office

U.S. Department of Health and Human Services: *The Health Benefits of Smoking Cessation. A Report of the Surgeon General.* U.S. Department of Health and Human Services, Public Health Service, Office on Smoking and Health, 1990.

———*The Health Consequences of Smoking for Women.* A Report of the Surgeon General. U.S. Department of Health and Human Services, Public Health Service, Office of the Assistant Secretary for Health, Office on Smoking and Health, 1980.

———*Reducing the Health Consequences of Smoking—25 Years of Progress.* A Report of the Surgeon General. U.S. Department of Health and Human Services, Public Health Service, Office on Smoking and Health, 1989.

———*The Health Consequences of Smoking: Nicotine Addiction.* A Report of the Surgeon General. U.S. Department of Health and Human Services, Public Health Service. Office on Smoking and Health, 1988.

Wack, J. T. and Rodin, J. "Smoking and its Effects on Body Weight and the Systems of Caloric Regulation." *American Journal of Clinical Nutrition,* 35 (1982): 366–380.

Notes

Notes

Notes

Notes

Notes

Notes

Notes

Notes

Notes

Notes

Notes

Notes

Notes

6/97